Father John,

Thanks for the encouragement and inspiration

Martin Nkafu

2013

From San Cataldo to Pittston

The Ormando Family in the Wyoming Valley

Martin Novak

From San Cataldo to Pittston
The Ormando Family in the Wyoming Valley
Copyright © 2013 by Martin Novak

All rights reserved. No part of this book may be reproduced or transmitted in any form or by any means without written permission from the author.

ISBN-13: 978-1489522030

Printed in USA by CreateSpace

Table of Contents

Preface 1

Dedication 2

1 – Sicily 4

2 – Coming to America 15

3 – Where They Settled 21

4 – Challenges They Faced 28

5 – How They Lived 41

6 – The Family at Home 51

7 – Biographical Vignettes 61

    Nellie Amico 62
    Angelo Occhipenti 66
    Stephen Bellanca 68
    Ross Prizzi 71
    Tony Amico 73
    Concetto "Frank" Agati 76
    Mary DiLorenzo 80
    Catal Ormando 84
    Lucille Leonardi 87

8 – Remains 92

9 – Epilogue 95

Afterword 97

Appendix – Pedigree Charts 99

    Pedigree Chart for Nellie Amico 100
    Pedigree Chart for Stephen Bellanca 101
    Pedigree Chart for Ross Prizzi 102
    Pedigree Chart for Mary DiLorenzo 103
    Pedigree Chart for Catal Ormando 104
    Pedigree Chart for Lucille Leonardi 105

Pedigree Chart for Martin Novak (author) 106

Descendants of Gaetano Ormando 107

First Generation 107
Second Generation 108
Third Generation 112

Author's Notes 122

Bibliography 123

Online Databases 123
Periodicals 124
Books 125
Web sites, e-sources 126
Unpublished Sources 129
Vital Records 129
Legal Sources 129

Acknowledgements 130

Table of Figures 131

Index 133

Endnotes 137

Preface

"Do not oppress an alien; you yourselves know how it feels to be aliens, because you were aliens in Egypt." Exodus 23:9

Between 1903 and 1914, twenty members of the Ormando family made the journey from San Cataldo, Sicily to Pittston, Pennsylvania. Most of those who came left loved ones behind that they would never see again. The family members were either sulfur miners, or peasant farmers. They were all poor. In coming to America, they were looking for a better life – if not for themselves, then for their future generations.

This is the story of why they came to America, the challenges they faced as immigrants, how they lived, and the family traditions that supported them. Many of their experiences were the same as other Sicilians that immigrated to America to find work in Pennsylvania's coalfields. Some of their stories were unique. The biographical vignettes highlight some of those unique experiences.

Nestled in the heart of Luzerne County is the Wyoming Valley. Formed over millions of years by the movement of the earth, the Susquehanna River runs through the valley. This valley possesses a unique beauty, and for some it is home for generation after generation.

My Sicilian ancestors came to the Wyoming Valley and settled into several of the many towns that dot the landscape. Places like Wyoming, Wilkes-Barrè, Scranton, Exeter, Yatesville, Browntown, Dallas, Harvey's Lake, and Pittston were where the Ormando family settled and many of their descendants still reside.

Martin Novak
May 2013

Dedication

I remember as a kid walking with my grandfather, siblings, and several of my cousins to Ristagno's Grocery Store. There, my grandfather, Gaetano Leonardi, treated us to bubblegum, and penny candy and whatever else we wanted.

You see, "Papa" as we used to call him, needed what seemed like a long walk to us (it was only a block), so the he could have enough time to smoke one of the cigars he so loved. He was not supposed to smoke them, as he had developed emphysema from working in and around the coalmines for many years. Papa never spoke in English to us much, but he knew everything that was going on in our lives. Language was never a barrier to understanding for him.

My grandmother, Mary Ormando, never completed more than four years of schooling, but was smart as a whip. Her English was excellent, and her grammar was impeccable. How she managed that with a fourth-grade education is beyond my understanding. We called her "Mama."

Mama had her favorite sayings, like "si dispone di mezza testa," which means you have half a head. That was her way of letting you know you had done something not so smart.

I recall visiting with my Aunt Josephine across town and her always having food, and lots of it. Even if we had just had dinner at my grandmother's house, there was always more food to be eaten. I remember her husband, John Adonizio, sitting in his easy chair rooting for his University of Pittsburgh Panthers. Tony Dorsett played for them then, and they were good.

Mostly, I remember spending the holidays in Pittston, Pennsylvania with my grandparents, cousins and aunts and uncles. Invariably, extended family would stop by and the adults would catch up on all the latest news, while we kids played.

Papa died in September 1973 from emphysema. He did live long enough for him and Mary to celebrate their 50th wedding anniversary on 15 July 1973. That was the first funeral that I remember going to. It was hard to believe that such a gentle, kind man was gone.

My grandmother lived until October 1989 in constant pain from rheumatoid arthritis. I remember her daughters – my mother and aunts – lamenting her death, yet consoled that now she would be able to dance again. Mama loved to dance when she was a young woman.

It is to them that I dedicate this work.

For all you did for us…Ti amo.

1 - Gaetano and Mary Ormando Leonardi at their home at 225 S. Main Street in Pittston, Pennsylvania, circa 1965

1 – Sicily

ON THE ISLAND OF SICILY, are the provinces of Trapani, Agrigento, Ragusa, Siracusa, Messina, Palermo, Enna, Catania, and Caltanissetta.

The province of Caltanissetta covers an area of 822 square miles, and contains 22 municipalities, or *comuni*, including Montedoro, Serradifalco, and San Cataldo. The Ormando family was from the city of San Cataldo.

San Cataldo was founded in 1607 by Lord Nicolo Galletti. It is named after its patron saint, Saint Cataldas. On 18 September 1865, San Cataldo became a city by Royal Decree number 2519 from King Vittorio Emmanuelle II of Italy.[1]

In the late 1800s, Caltanissetta was the center of the Sicilian Sulfur industry, and held the head offices for the mines as well as a school for mining surveyors.

Indeed, very crude methods were used to extract the sulfur from these mines, though the yield was often quite good. In 1900 alone, the export of raw sulfur from Caltanissetta was 557,668 tons.[2] Sulfur mining, though, was cruel, back-breaking work. Mining was done by hand, in spaces that were often too small for a man to stand. Hauling sulfur out of the mines meant equally narrow passage ways to the surface. For this purpose, children were made to be slave workers.

Child slave labor was rampant. In a land where families were poor with many children to feed, unscrupulous mine owners preyed upon the youth. In his expose "The Man Farthest Down – Child Labor and the Sulfur Mines," Booker T. Washington compared the plight of the child slave laborers in Sicily to that of the African-Americans enslaved in the United States prior to the Civil War. He thought they were worse off than their American counterparts.

Accidents occurred regularly in the Sicilian sulfur mines. Common injuries included broken limbs due to stone falling from roofs, and conjunctivitis from sulfuric acid in the air. Death could occur from falling down mine shafts, being crushed during cave-ins, and asphyxiation from inhaling carbon dioxide gases. Long lives were a rarity among the sulfur miners of Sicily.

The brutal lives of the Sicilian sulfur miners in the at the turn of the 20th Century were strikingly similar to that of the American coalminers. Sicilian sulfur miners, though were much poorer than their American counterparts. The men and boys of the Ormando family learned their mining trade in the Sicilian sulfur mines. Most all would one day become coalminers in America.

THE SPIRIT OF *CAMPANILISMO* was strong throughout Sicily in the late 19th Century. Although it has no direct translation into English, the word parochial captures the meaning of it. *Campanilismo* conveys a sense of belonging to one's own town or village (e.g., San Cataldo), accompanied with a narrow view of the outside world. This parochialism continued for the Ormando family when they immigrated to America.

The people in Sicily struggled to make a living in trying circumstances. The government in Rome, that did little to modernize Sicily, nevertheless extracted taxes and imposed their laws. The Roman Catholic Church, the dominant religion in Italy, also collected money from the people of Sicily from church offerings to alms for penance.

The Sicilians held on to their traditions and their folklore, long after they became obsolete in Northern Italy. Together, these forces made the Sicilian's plight a difficult one indeed. No matter how hard they tried, they would never get ahead.

2 - Map of Sicily, with location of San Cataldo circled. (William Agnew Paton, 1897)

THOUGH THE GOVERNMENT of Italy had always played a role in the lives of Sicilians, 1861 marked a turning point in history of Italy. Prior to that time, Italy had been a collection of independent kingdoms and quasi-republics. It was in 1861 that Giuseppe Garibaldi united Italy under one government. That government would be in Rome.

With the unification, the differences between northern and southern Italy came into sharper focus. While in Northern Italy, society was progressing socially, economically and politically, the same could not be said for the *Il Mezzogiorno*, or Southern Italy.[3] Sicilians, in particular, were seen as backwards by their northern counterparts.

The northern cities of Italy, including Venice, Rome, and Florence had schools, cities with modern amenities, farms that flourished, and most importantly, jobs. Southern Italy was a relic of another age. Many of its farms were barren, and its politics were feudal.

The realities of how much needed to be done by the new government were overwhelming. There were no roads, railways, or other reliable means of navigation throughout Sicily. An organized school system did not yet exist. Towns and cities did not have means to provide sanitation and clean water for their residents.

All of these problems required money. A system of taxation was put in place to "address" these issues. However, to the Sicilians it seemed that a great deal of their money was going to places in Italy other than Sicily. In addition, a unified Italy required Sicilian men for her army.

This created a growing resentment in Southern Italy toward a government that took their money with excessive taxes, and conscripted their men into the army. These actions took much of the capital and labor away from Southern Italy, and had a devastating impact on its economy.

In Sicily, relatively few families controlled all of the usable land for agriculture. This system was called *Latifondi*[4] in Sicily, or Estates in Sicily. Methods of farming were crude, and all done by hand. One-half of all the peasant's earnings were taken by the landowners for rent. If the peasant farmer did have a bountiful harvest, there were customs duties to pay.

The rate of absentee landowners was high, due to their interest only in making profit, and not in the usability of the land. The landowners also had no interest in improving their properties, lest their taxes on the land increase.

Economic conditions worsened for the southern Italians in the period between 1870 and 1900, with the cost of food accounting for seventy-five percent of their available income. What they had was insufficient for their survival, and undernourishment was rampant in southern Italy. An agricultural crisis in 1880 made a bad situation even worse.

If this was not enough, to add to the Sicilian's misery cholera epidemic killed about 55,000 people in 1887. Finally, in 1903, phylloxera devastated the grape crops in Sicily. Related to aphids, phylloxera are microscopic in size, yet lay waste to grape crops during an infestation. It was estimated that over 900 Italian provinces were infested, and more than 700,000 acres were destroyed by this pestilence.[5] Together, these conditions made immigration to America an inescapable conclusion for a large portion of the Sicilian population.

THE VIEW OF THE SICILIAN toward religion was complex. In Sicily, there were three distinct attitudes concerning spiritual life, including "the devout Roman Catholics, the majority of whom consist of peasants, largely illiterate, plus the decreasing...noblemen who give themselves to an ecclesiastical career, and the clergy. [There were] a smaller number of freethinkers, agnostics, atheists, and materialists, for the most part workingmen in large cities and professional men. [Finally, there were] the millions, apparently indifferent who go through life without religious feeling or spiritual experience."[6]

Regardless of the varying attitudes toward spirituality, the Roman Catholic Church has long been the dominant religion in Sicily. The relationship between the church and its people has evolved over time.

The church first played the role of converter, for the people of Sicily worshiped pagan gods before Christianity was known to them. The Roman Catholic Church at times was both a place of worship and the seat of government. Regardless of the role played by the church, the relationship between the people of Sicily and the church has often been uneasy.

For the people of Sicily, the church became – like the government – yet another monolithic institution with its teachings and beliefs that were to be followed if one wanted to be a "good" Catholic. Sicilians, often poor and living off the land, viewed the church with suspicion. This was especially true with regard to the clergy, who the people often viewed as corrupt and indifferent to their strife.

IT WAS THE MARTYRS AND SAINTS of the church that gave religion a human face to the people struggling to live in Sicily. The people could relate to them, and pray to them for relief from sickness, or protection from evil.

Of all the saints, the one who most humanized the Roman Catholic Church was Mary, the Blessed Mother of Jesus. The center of worship in San Cataldo was the *Nativity of Mary*, better known as the *Mother Church*.

The original *Mother Church* was completed in 1632. A devastating fire in 1788 caused the church to loose most of its early parish records. There are three naves in the church and at one time held 14 altars.[7]

Within the *Mother Church* are several chapels, including the *Oratory of the Blessed Sacrament*, from the 18th century; the *Oratory*, founded in 1654; *Saint Anthony Abbot*; *San Giuseppe*, housing a bell tower; and the *Lord of the Mysteries*, which was destroyed during World War II.[8]

The *Mother Church* is also the seat of the parish of Santa Maria del Rosario. Contained within this parish is the church of *Santa Lucia*.

The Church of *Santa Lucia* was founded in the early 18th century, though there are records to indicate that it may have existed in some form in the prior century. Each year on the December 13, the saint day of St. Lucia, it becomes a destination of many devoted pilgrims. The Church of *Santa Lucia* also played an important role in the story of the Ormando family, as all of their pre-immigrant baptisms and weddings were held there.

PIOUS DEVOTION to the Madonna and canonized individuals was commonplace in southern and Eastern Europe, but the "cult of the saints" was especially strong in rural southern Italy. Each Italian village had its own patron saint that, residents believed, would watch over them and act as an intermediary between them and God.

Besides the routine veneration of their saintly patrons, villagers paid homage in grand style on the saint's annual feast day. The yearly fiesta began with villagers packing the church to hear Mass and a tribute to the patron saint.

The religious services over, people joined in a massive procession that included brass bands and an enormous statue of the saint. Crowds chanted as the figure was ceremoniously carried through village streets.

The annual daylong fiesta characteristically took on a festival atmosphere. Vendors' stands lined the streets; people ate, drank, danced, sang, gambled, and joined in various other entertainments. Fireworks displays drew the days' celebrations to a close. Because every village had a patron, competition among villages to outdo one another's public adulation of their saints contributed to the spectacular, even ostentatious, nature of the fiesta. Italian immigrants naturally brought the cherished tradition of the annual fiesta with them to the United States.[9]

The most venerated saint in San Cataldo is Saint Cataldo. Every May 10 the people of San Cataldo hold a procession in honor of Saint Cataldo. The celebration begins with a solemn vespers on May 9 along with the anniversary of dedication of the mother church. On the morning of May 10, there is gunfire in the early morning to announce the celebration.

The *Mother Church* celebrates masses through the morning and into the afternoon. Then the church, presided by the archpriest, concelebrated by all the priests of the city, and followed by townspeople, hold a solemn procession through the main streets of San Cataldo.

To outsiders, the reverence, pomp, and circumstance might remind some of a pagan rite. However, one must remember why Cataldus from Ireland became so venerated a saint in Italy.

CATALDUS, IS KNOWN as the *Shipwrecked Saint*. St. Cataldus of Taranto, Italy, was a holy man who was appointed Bishop in Lismore, County Waterford, Ireland in the eighth century. After serving some time there, he made a pilgrimage to the Holy Land.

It was on his return to Ireland that he became shipwrecked off the southern coast of Italy. There, Cataldus had an epiphany and resolved to stay amongst the pagan people of the area and convert them to Christianity.

Cataldus performed his missionary work in the Taranto area of Italy, which lies at the boot heel of the country. It was within a few years that the people of the area named him their bishop.

Cataldus is the patron saint against blindness, epilepsy, drought, paralysis, and plague. He is also the saint protector of San Cataldo, and over 150 churches in Italy bear his name.

THE ORMANDO FAMILY WERE much like other Sicilian families in the 1880s and 1890s, which did not enjoy the rise in quality of life that the people in other areas of Italy experienced in the late 19th century. In fact, their poverty was often to the point of destitution, with little hope for a better future.

3- Gaetano Ormando, patriarch of the Ormando family, circa 1906. Courtesy of Vince Aquilina.

THE PATRIARCH OF THE ORMANDO FAMILY, Gaetano Ormando, was born 24 August 1848 to Giuseppe and Giuseppa Ormando. He married Grazia "Grace" Occhipenti on 3 August 1873 in the church of Santa Lucia in San Cataldo, Sicily.[10] Grace Occhipenti was born 14 July 1856 to Giovanni and Lucia Amico Occhipenti.

The couple had nine children. With the exception of the three children that died in infancy, the other children of Gaetano and Grace Ormando came to America.

Sometimes, Sicilians emigrated by themselves with the hope of earning enough money to finance their family's passage later. Often, entire families emigrated leaving behind what they knew for the hope that awaited them in America.

For those who married into the Ormando family, this meant leaving behind their mothers, fathers, siblings and other relatives whom they would most likely never see again. Mary Ormando Leonardi, then in her eighties, cried when remembering the relatives that her family had to leave behind in Sicily to come to America.

As with the Ormando family, many times extended families emigrated and settled into their new country living in the same neighborhoods. This enabled them to rely on one another in their new country as they had in Sicily. Their parochial views - the *campanilismo* – came with them to America as well.

Why they chose to come to America was likely similar to the thousands of other Italians who emigrated from Italy in the mass migration between 1880 and 1920 – to escape the extreme poverty of southern Italy in the hopes of a better life in America.

Therefore, they came to America.

Ormando Family Overview

1-Gaetano Ormando (24 Aug 1848-6 Feb 1929)
+Grazia "Grace" Occhipenti (14 Jul 1856-26 Dec 1923)
   Married – 3 Aug 1873

. . . 2-Giuseppe "Joseph" Ormando (5 Apr 1876-15 May 1951)
. . . +Grazia "Grace" Grifasi (28 Nov 1884-20 Mar 1942)
   Married – 15 Sep 1900

. . . 2-Giuseppa "Josephine" Ormando (2 Mar 1879-28 Jun 1947)
. . . +Cataldo Amico (25 Oct 1870-9 Aug 1961)
   Married – 13 Jun 1896

. . . 2-Lucia "Lucy" Ormando (15 Oct 1882-6 Apr 1952)
. . . +Salvatore "Sam" Prizzi (12 Feb 1877-2 Apr 1956)
   Married – 16 Dec 1899

. . . 2-Maria Ormando (28 June 1885-Dec 1885)

. . . 2-Giovanni "John" Ormando (30 Jan 1888-Mar 1964)
. . . +Rosaria "Sara" Pilato (16 Feb 1892-Oct 1970)
   Married – 10 Dec 1910

. . . 2-Salvatore Ormando (4 Aug 1890-11 Sep 1892)

. . . 2-Salvatore Ormando (28 Feb 1893-3 Nov 1893)

. . . 2-Maria "Mary" Ormando (9 Jun 1895-18 Feb 1980)
. . . +Concetto "Frank" Agati (11 Jun 1888-16 Feb 1928)
   Married – 6 Feb 1910

. . . 2-Rosina "Rose" Ormando (26 Oct 1898-5 Jun 1973)
. . . +Salvatore "Sam" Bellanca (19 Jan 1887-4 Aug 1951)
   Married - 1913

4 - The Ormando siblings that came to America, from left – John, Rose, Josephine, Lucy, Maria, and Joseph. Circa 1942. Courtesy of Vince Aquilina

2 – Coming to America

The decision to leave one's homeland could not have been easy to make. Travelling to one's port of departure could be perilous. The voyage across the Atlantic would be difficult with cramped living quarters. As we shall see, arriving at Ellis Island was no insurance that the voyage would be successful. Despite many obstacles, immigrants came by the millions to seek a better life for themselves and their future generations.

Cui cerca, trova; cui sècuta, vinci.
  Who seeks finds; who perseveres, wins – An old Sicilian proverb

THE PASSAGE TO AMERICA was not the pleasant image of a cruise, as we know it today. In 1904, passage to America from Sicily would have cost about $40 (about $1,025 in 2012). Prior to boarding their boat to America, prospective immigrants had to pass through a barrage of questions by Italian inspectors mandated by the United States Government:

- Were they married?
- Could they read or write?
- Where did they live in Italy?
- Name and address of the person they were to join in America.
- Had they ever been in prison?
- Who paid for their passage?
- Were they polygamists or anarchists?
- Were they carrying at least $50?

If they made it this far, they were inoculated for small pox, still a very real health danger at the close of the 19th century. Then, it was onto the medical inspection. In no particular order, the doctors looked for signs of eye disease, or fungus-like diseases. Finally, after surviving this de-humanizing process, an immigrant could board their intended ship.

Most Italian immigrants from Sicily came via third class, or steerage. Once onboard the vessel, the immigrant's lodgings were cramped, and they had no privacy. Beds were generally iron bunks, with straw for a mattress, no pillows, or sheets, with a tattered blanket. These blankets were typically washed between voyages, but the filthiness was everywhere.

Third-class passengers also did not have access to a dining room or eating utensils. They had to eat their meals in their living quarters. Garbage ended up on the floor, as there were no trash receptacles in steerage. Passengers in steerage also shared common toilet facilities.

Occasionally, an Italian inspector would make the voyage to ensure that the conditions for passengers in steerage were livable. "Said one emigrant, who had had an experience of more than one voyage across the Atlantic, 'When the [Italian Inspector] is on board, the steerage is heaven; when he is absent, it is hell.' " [1]

At the beginning of the twentieth century, the average trip took about ten days, covering some 3,100 nautical miles between Palermo (the usual point of departure) and New York's Ellis Island (the usual point of arrival). Yet, arriving was no insurance that one would necessarily make it to one's intended destination.

EVERY IMMIGRANT HAD TO PASS a gauntlet prior to admission. One portion of it included the dreaded eye exam, used to detect trachoma.[2] The invasive means to detect trachoma meant that trauma and pain would be one of the examined person's first experiences in America. The common practice for detecting trachoma in the early 20th century was "on making the patient look down, seize the [eye lash] with the thumb and forefinger of one hand, and draw the lid firmly downward away from the [eye]. With the other hand place a glass rod, or thin pencil on the part of the lid which lies over the convex border of the tarsus and adjoining fornix; push it well downward, without pressing on the [eye] and at the same time raise the [eyelid] as quickly as possible."[3] In practice at Ellis Island, the instrument used to push down was a button-hook.

Immigrants could also be detained or excluded for dysentery, tuberculosis, mental retardation, or poor eyesight. Relatively few immigrants were turned away upon medical inspection. Between 1910 and 1915, only 36,074 out of 5,501,401 immigrants were detained or excluded. The majority of those were for contagious diseases.[4]

Immigrants arriving at Ellis Island were expected to have enough money such that they could pay their own way. They were also expected to have cash for transportation and sustenance until the immigrant could find work. Unless the newly arrived had at least twenty-five dollars, officials at Ellis Island could declare that such an immigrant would likely be a charity case.

One must bear in mind that $25 in 1910 was a lot of money, even for those already living in America (today that $25 is equivalent to about $610). There was no welfare system in the United States during the wave of immigration between 1900 and 1920, so the fear of immigrants becoming public charges was perceived to be real.

In reality, very few Italians became a public burden. At the beginning of the 20th Century, less than 2% of beggars in New York City were Italian immigrants.[5] To the Sicilian immigrants, a job – no matter how menial – was better than taking a handout.

5 - Arriving at Ellis Island. Library Of Congress, Prints And Photographs Division

ACCORDING TO GAETANO ORMANDO'S RESPONSES on the 1910 United States Census, he arrived in 1870.[6] Though no records have been located that prove this claim, no records have been found that dispute the claim either. If he did come to the United States in 1870, it is likely that Gaetano was a "bird of passage."

Birds of passage were those immigrants who were planning to return to Italy for one reason or another. Sometimes these birds of passage were seasonal workers, who returned to Italy once a harvest was completed if they were farm workers. Others returned to Italy once they had found work and a place for their families to live. It is likely that Gaetano was the latter form of the bird of passage. Why another 30 years passed before the family came to America permanently is a mystery.

CATALDO AMICO, the husband of Josephine Ormando, arrived at Ellis Island on 10 May 1902 on the vessel *Bolivia*.[7] It is likely that the family pooled their resources for Cataldo to purchase the initial homestead in Pittston. For, over the next few years, several members of the family would name 18 Price Street as their destination when they made their way through Ellis Island.

The next member of the family to immigrate was Sam Prizzi, the husband of Lucy Ormando. He arrived on 11 March 1903 on the vessel *Trojan Prince*. Noted on the ship's manifest was the Sam would be staying with Cataldo Amico at 18 Price Street in Pittston.[8]

On 9 July 1903, on the vessel *Citta di Napoli*, Josephine Ormando Amico arrived at Ellis Island with her daughter Nellie. With them were Lucy Ormando Prizzi, and her son Anthony. Their destination was 18 Price Street in Pittston.[9]

Joseph Ormando and his brother John arrived on 27 March 1904 on the vessel *Citta di Milano*. Both were denied entry.[10]

Frank Agati, the soon-to-be husband of Mary Ormando, arrived on 23 March 1907 aboard the *Sofia Hohnberg*. He too would make his way to 18 Price Street in Pittston.[11]

After returning to Italy, Lucy Ormando Prizzi brought her daughter Anna and sons Anthony and Ross to America on 22 July 1909 aboard the *Principe Di Piemonte*. They joined Sam Prizzi at their family home at 107 South Main Street in Pittston.[12]

The patriarch of the family Gaetano Ormando and his wife Grace Occhipenti, and their daughters Mary and Rose Ormando arrived on 19 August 1909 on the vessel *Regina d'Italia*. Their final destination was 18 Price Street in Pittston.[13]

By 1910, twelve Ormando family members had immigrated to America. Immigration would continue for the family in 1911.

John Ormando and his wife, Sara Pilato, would arrive on the *Venezia* on 30 March 1911. Both were denied entry.[14] John would attempt to enter the United States again on 13 April 1911 on the vessel *Sant' Anna*. This time he was admitted.[15] Sara would attempt to enter the United States a second time on 23 February 1913 aboard the vessel *Canada*. She would once again be denied entry.[16]

Sara Pilato and her brother in-law, Joseph Ormando, would enter the United States legally through the Canadian border on 9 July 1913. When they entered the country at Vanceboro, Maine, it was noted that Joseph's legal address was 5 West Oak Street in Pittston, Pennsylvania.[17] Sara Pilato's tenacity and perseverance were admirable. To be denied entry three times, and try yet again was truly remarkable.

Sam Bellanca, husband of Rose Ormando, arrived on 24 October 1913 aboard the *Virginia*. Sam too made his way to Pittston to join his wife Rose Ormando at 9 West Oak Street.[18]

On 11 June 1914, Grace Grifasi, wife of Joseph Ormando arrived aboard the vessel *Sant' Anna*, along with her daughters, Grace and Mary, and her sons Anthony, and Catal.[19] Together, they would they would be the last members of the Ormando family born in Sicily to immigrate to America.

The average age for all members of the Ormando family that immigrated from 1903 through 1913 was 19.9, with the youngest being Anthony Prizzi in 1903 at one year old, and the oldest being the patriarch, Gaetano Ormando, at 61 years of age in 1909.

On every passenger manifest, prospective immigrants had to indicate their final destination. Without exception, the members of the Ormando family indicated that Pittston, Pennsylvania was their destination.

DURING THE YEARS that the family immigrated, there were few, if any cars. Getting from New York City to Pittston meant taking a train on the *Delaware, Lackawanna, and Western Railroad (DLWR) – Lackawanna Limited Line*. Leaving at 10:00am from the DLWR terminal in Hoboken, New Jersey, passengers could expect to arrive in Scranton, Pennsylvania by 2:00pm.[20] From there, passengers would take the *Laurel Line* from Scranton to Pittston. Passengers could expect that their total time in transit would be about six hours.

3 – Where They Settled

Where Italian immigrants settled depended on the labor skills they possessed. If they were steelworkers, they could find work in steel mills of Pennsylvania and Ohio. Barbers could ply their trade in any of the cities along the Eastern Seaboard. Those with butchering skills often made their way to the meat packing plants near Chicago. If the newcomers had tailoring skills, they often settled in the garment district of New York City.

If they had worked in the sulfur mines in Sicily, Italian immigrants headed for the coalfields in West Virginia and Pennsylvania. The Ormando family settled in the Wyoming Valley of Luzerne County, Pennsylvania.

LUZERNE COUNTY WAS FOUNDED on 25 September 1786, and was formed from portions of Northumberland County. The county was named for Chevalier del la Luzerne, the second minister from France to the United States, who served from 1779 – 1784.

When originally formed, the county consisted of eleven townships, including Wilkes-Barre, Hanover, Pittston, Exeter, Newport, Kingston, Plymouth, Salem, Tioga, Wyalusing, and Tunkhannock. The original boundaries of the townships were also extended when Luzerne County was formed.

6 - Map of Luzerne, Lackawanna, and Wyoming Counties, circa 1880

The total size of the county has been reduced several times through annexation. In 1804, a portion of the county was annexed to form Lycoming County; Susquehanna and Bradford Counties were created through annexation again in 1810. In 1842, Wyoming County was annexed from Luzerne. Finally, Lackawanna County was annexed in 1878 to bring Luzerne County to its present borders.

THE WYOMING VALLEY is a beautiful area in the Appalachian mountain chain, nestled in the heart of Luzerne County, Pennsylvania. Before the discovery of coal, the area was a remote destination from other areas of Pennsylvania or New York. It was the discovery of coal that brought the system of canals, and later the railroads, to the area. This accessibility led to an influx of population to the area, and the development of coal resources led to tremendous wealth in the region.

The abundance of coal mining opportunities led immigrants to the Wyoming Valley. These opportunities held the promise of a better life for themselves and their descendants. Much of the American Industrial Revolution was fueled by the Anthracite coal mined in the Wyoming Valley.[21]

The existence of coal in the Wyoming Valley had been known as early as 1768, when Obadiah and Daniel Gore opened a mine near Wilkes-Barre.[22] The anthracite coal discovered in northeastern Pennsylvania was much harder than the bituminous coal found in West Virginia and Western Pennsylvania. There was uncertainty as to whether this new type of coal would be useful.

It was 1808 when Jessie Fell recorded his experiments of burning coal in an open grate. That year, in the Free Mason's Monitor, he wrote "February 11, [1808]. Made the experiment of burning the common stone coal of the valley in a grate in a common fireplace in my house, and find it will answer the purpose of fuel, making a clearer and better fire, at less expense, than burning wood in the common way."[23]

Thus, it was discovered that the anthracite coal would burn longer and hotter, making it ideal for home and industrial use. Thereafter, the tonnage of coal mined and sold continued to increase, from a total of 174,743 tons in 1830 to 26,142,089 tons in 1879.[24]

King coal was flourishing in Northeastern Pennsylvania. It appeared that there was much profit to be made, and the abundant labor could be hired for low wages.

When John Emerson Marble wrote about the coal industry in his 1880 book, *The History of Luzerne, Lackawanna, and Wyoming Counties*, he prophetically warned of trouble ahead. "The exercise of all the good sense of parties concerned will be needed to secure the trade from loss in the future. Disaster may come from too sudden prosperity, as to the apparently convalescent patient from an excess of vitality. Prices must be regulated, or the goose that lays the golden egg may be killed."[25] Time would tell how portentous his warning would become.

VILLAGES AND TOWNS sprung up throughout the area as immigrants came to the Wyoming Valley. Townships and villages in the greater Pittston area included Browntown, Cork Lane, Hughestown, Port Griffith, and Sebastapol. The most important of these to the Ormando family was the city of Pittston.

Approximately halfway between Scranton to the northeast and Wilkes-Barre to the southwest, lies the greater Pittston area. Pittston was named for the British Statesman, Sir William Pitt the Elder. It includes the townships and boroughs of Exeter, Duryea, Jenkins, Hughestown, Pittston Township, West Pittston, West Wyoming, Wyoming, and Yatesville.

The abundance of coal in and near Pittston led to its prosperity. Many of the companies that would become synonymous with King Coal were formed there by 1875, including the *Pennsylvania Coal Company*, *Lehigh Valley Company*, *Pittston Coal Company*, and the *Hillside Coal and Iron Company*.

In August of 1850, the *Pittston Gazette* began circulation that would last until 1900. The paper would resurface again as the *Gazette*, and would last until late 1965. Aside from heralding the news of the day, the paper also focused on the industrial topics of importance to the Pittston area – Coal, iron, textiles, terra cotta works, and breweries.

Banks were needed to accommodate the prosperity of the area. On 5 May 1857, the *Pittston Bank* was incorporated. On 1 November 1869, the *Miner's Savings Bank* opened for business. The *People's Savings Bank* was incorporated on 1 April 1872. Finally, the *First National Bank* followed on 6 July 1874.[26]

Pittston also lays claim to the first public school in the Wyoming Valley. By 1880, there were twelve public schools within the Pittston Township, along with twenty-one within the Pittston borough. The growing demand for coal, abundance of industry, along with the infrastructure in place, would attract a multitude of immigrants to the Pittston area over the next 35 years.

7 - Pittston, circa 1907. Library of Congress, Prints and Photographs Division

By 1915, there were approximately 60,000 people living in the greater Pittston area. There was an array of anthracite coalmines, and other industries, including silk mills, iron and terra cotta works, machine shops, brass foundries, cigar factories, dress factories, silk manufacturers, and engine works. The banks in the Pittston area boasted combined deposits of $8,000,000. There were 40,000 railroad freight cars annually leaving from and arriving in Pittston. Sixty-thousand people visited her via automobile or bus every year.[27] It was a lively; thriving community that welcomed the Ormando family to America.

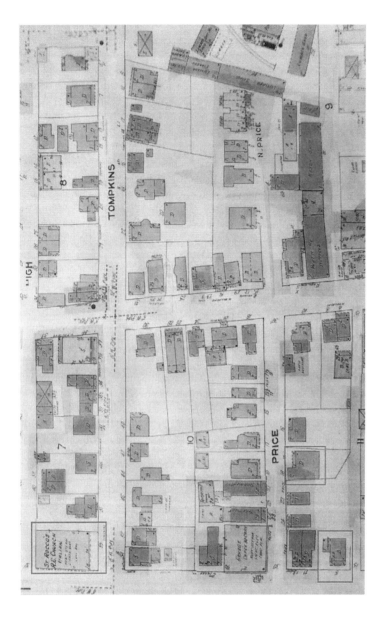

8 - Section of Pittston, 11th Ward, circa 1930 - Highlighted are 5 West Oak Street, home of Joseph Ormando; 18 Price Street, home of Cataldo Amico; and Saint Rocco's Church Courtesy of The Luzerne County Historical Society

4 – Challenges They Faced

Italian immigrants faced a myriad of challenges not the least of which was a language barrier. My ancestors did not read or speak English. For their part, Americans did not seem interested in helping immigrants to bridge the language barrier. The new immigrants were called "wops" or "dagos" and ridiculed for their inability to speak English.

Economic hardships were another unpleasant fact for Italian immigrants. They generally had large families, women did not work outside of the home, and the wages for the men were meager. Having enough money to pay rent and pay for food was difficult. There were no vacations, or sick leave, and extravagances were few.

Italian immigrants were also lacking in routine healthcare – the kind of preventive medicine that we take for granted. The southern Italians, in particular, had a basic distrust of doctors, priests, lawyers, and government officials. Conditioned to mistrust public officials in Italy, it was very difficult to reverse this tradition in America.

THE WORKING CONDITIONS for the first and second generations of the Ormando family were appalling. Overworked, overcrowded, underpaid, and unappreciated were the reality for the workers of the Ormando family. The effect of child labor also cannot be underestimated. Several members of the second generation of the Ormando family were working ten-hour days at nine years of age as breaker boys.[1]

In the first decade following their immigration, the Ormando family faced a job market that was not concerned about their safety. Working conditions for the average worker were dreadful, and often dangerous. It was a time when men like Henry Ford, and John D. Rockefeller were the titans of industry. For blue-collar workers, the dangers of their circumstances were underscored in the Triangle Shirt Waist Factory Fire on 25 March 1911.

One hundred, forty-six workers, mostly women, died in that fire. Subsequent investigations revealed that there were inadequate exits. Several exits were locked, and the lone fire escape collapsed under the weight of humanity trying to escape. Finally, there was a woeful lack of fire extinguishing apparatus available.

This proved to be a deadly combination for the workers of the factory trapped on the eighth and ninth floors of the building. Many of the deaths were due to victims desperately jumping from the windows, rather than burning to death. The fact that all of the management on site survived only punctuated the difference between worker and management.

It was common in the 1910s for an American worker to die on the job. Miners were always in danger of falling victim to roof collapses or explosions. Steelworkers could easily perish from molten steel pouring onto them. Workers in manufacturing industries were often chopped, dragged, or crushed by the very machinery that they worked on every day.

Workplace safety regulation was unheard of, and the few places it did exist were undermined by corrupt inspectors and a system that valued profit far more than the mortality of its workers. In the Wyoming Valley of Pennsylvania, coalmine operators took a similar view of their workers.

THE WYOMING VALLEY between 1900 and 1920 contained a multitude of coalmines, owned by companies such as the Volpe Coal Company, Pennsylvania Coal Company, Black Diamond Breaker, and Duryea Anthracite among them. Every male from the first generation of the Ormando family in America, with the exception of Frank Agati, worked in the coalmines.[2]

Joseph Ormando worked for the Pennsylvania Coal Company at their #5 Slope Colliery.[3] Sam Prizzi worked at the Eight Slope Colliery for the Pennsylvania Coal Company in Inkerman, Pennsylvania.[4] John Ormando worked at the Number 14 Colliery of the Pennsylvania Coal Company.[5] Sam Bellanca worked for the Pennsylvania Coal Company at their number five colliery.[6] Similarly, Cataldo Amico worked in the mines until his retirement in 1931.[7]

Employment in the coalmines was brutal work. A typical day for a miner meant being underground for up to ten hours per day, for six days a week.

> Once miners entered the mineshaft, they did not exit until their shift ended. They ate, drank, and performed necessary bodily functions in the depths of the earth. The miners' day began the moment they started their descent to perhaps a thousand feet below the surface. Depending on the setup, in some mines a cage-"a flimsy, shaky elevator, devoid of walls or anything else ... [to] cling to "-transported the men "down into the darkness…At the end of this wobbly ride, they walked to their workstations. In sites without cage transport, miners wound their way on foot down into the deep black pit below.

Regardless of whether men walked the entire way or descended into the mines in a cage and continued on, the trek by foot was usually the same. Stooping to avoid overhangs [and] ... scrambling on hands and knees on paths covered with chunks of coal and slate, miners made their way through dark passages probably no more than five and a half feet high.

Before they could begin work, the men had to check overhead for loose slate, rock, or coal and construct temporary ceilings to protect themselves from falling debris. Realizing they were paid by the amount of coal they extracted or loaded onto cars, workers kept busy. With electric drills or handpicks, miners bored holes into the walls, prepared the deposits for blasting, and then detonated explosives. Common laborers cleaned away the rock and loaded coal into cars that transported it aboveground.

The harsh clack of explosives detonating, the rumble of loaded cars, the banging of implements against hard surfaces, and the clang of rock, slate, and coal being thrown around all combined to create an oppressive atmosphere. The dust and grit that pervaded underground mines added to the already grim conditions workers faced every day.

Mining was not only noisy, dirty, and strenuous work, it was dangerous. There was the constant threat of a cave-in. Besides these catastrophic collapses, volatile dusts and gases increased the likelihood of deadly explosions in coalmines. In addition to being on guard against falling slate and rock, miners had to be on the lookout for frayed electric cables-or 'live wires' as the workers dubbed them – that powered the electric drills."[8]

The miner's pay was meager compared to the laborious nature of their work. In 1916, the average wage for a miner was $15.30 per week. By 1919, their pay was a penurious $26.55 per week. Most miners' families had multiple children. It is no wonder, given the paucity of income that boys were often forced to start working as young as eight years old.

When a worker died in the coalmines, the company would bring the body – if they could find the body – to the house and lay it on the front door step. They would inform the wife that her husband was dead and ask if there were any male children in the house.

If the answer were affirmative, the child – regardless of age – would be expected to be at work the next day. If the answer was no, the family would be evicted, often immediately. This was a cold, harsh, and cruel business with no time for sympathy or grief. One anthracite coal miner summed up a miner's life, saying, "Yes, we can earn good wages here, if all goes well, but it is living at the end of the world. We miners are like men going to war. If we succeed in saving some money and getting out with our lives, we may say 'we have lived in the midst of death and have escaped.' "[9]

Many miners lived in patch-towns that were owned by the mines. The houses were built and owned by the mines, miners were paid with company scrip, and had to shop at company stores – the only ones that would accept company scrip.

This continued for many years, and did not abate until the miners began to organize under the leadership of people like John L. Lewis. Lewis would become a hero to many miners and their families for his efforts at organizing the workers, and obtaining better pay – with real money – and better working conditions.

> The Lackawanna Coal Mine Museum, located in Scranton, Pennsylvania runs tours of its retired mine. I was fortunate in 2003 to participate in one of these tours. After travelling backward in a mine car, at approximately a seventy-degree angle, one watches the sunlight above become a mere pinhole of light.
>
> Then, save for the electric lights in the mine, nothing but utter darkness. At one point, to give participants a sense of what life was like for coalminers, the lights are turned out. Not even your own hand can be seen in front of your face. It is a constant, cool 53 degrees in the mine. The tour guides provide a frank discussion on what life was like for the men who worked these mines.
>
> It was a relief to know that I would only be 300 feet beneath the surface of the earth for a short while. It was an immense relief to see the sun and sky reappear at the end of the tour.

If a man lived through the experience of working in the mines, that alone did not ensure a long life. Working in the coalmines could lead to health problems years after retirement. Long-term exposure to particulates, sulfur dioxide, benzene, and coal dust could well lead to Black Lung Disease, Emphysema, Anthracosilicosis, Renal failure, and congestive heart failure.

Many of the men in the Ormando family would have their lives affected or shortened due to these afflictions. Gaetano Leonardi would pass away in 1973 because of the Emphysema he developed resulting from his employment with the coal mining industry.

OBTAINING AN EDUCATION in the early 20th Century was no easy task. It was not until 1938, with the passage of the Fair Labor Standards Act, that minors were prohibited from working in conditions of oppressive employment. The Act also provided that children under the age of 16 could not be employed during school hours.

It is no surprise then that graduation rate for all 17 year-olds in the school year 1909 – 1910 was 8.8 per 100,000. By 1920, that rate was only 16.8 per 100,000. The percentage of 5 – 19 year-olds in 1910 attending school was 59.2%. That figure rose to 64.3% in 1920. For comparison, in 1991, 93.1% of the same age group was attending school.[10]

The median years of school completed in 1910 were 8.1 years (barely into 8th Grade). In 1920, the median was 8.2 years completed. It would not be until 1960 that the median years completed would rise above 10 years. Overall, at the beginning of the Twentieth Century, fewer children were attending school, while fewer still were graduating with a high school diploma. Only one percent of children from Italian families attended high school before 1920.

Thus, the first generation of Ormando family immigrants were at a great disadvantage with regard to education, averaging 2.7 years of schooling completed. Three never went to school at all. That they were able to provide for their families is a testament to their perseverance.

By 1944, when the last of the second generation of the Ormando family reached the age of 18, they were averaging 8.6 years of schooling completed. Anthony Prizzi, born in 1901, was the first of his generation to graduate from high school, and by 1940, he was a bank clerk.

Yet, other members of the second generation did not fare as well in obtaining an education. Anthony "Tony" Ormando, born in 1908, never attended school and was working in the mines by the age of nine. Mary Ormando, born in 1903, had attended school through the fourth grade while in Sicily. Since she did not speak English when she immigrated, she was forced to start school all over again beginning with the first grade. This was, unfortunately, typical for many immigrants.

Because their previous education was considered deficient or their English substandard, immigrant children in public schools might well be placed in classes with younger pupils. "These youngsters were labeled 'retarded,' which meant they were older than the normal age of students in their grade…As a result of the school systems' 'retardation' policies, young people found themselves forced into classes with children who might be about two-thirds their size and perhaps half their age. Recently arrived older boys and girls who could speak no English met the same fate."[11]

This must have been a painful and often lonely experience for immigrants that found they were strangers in a strange unaccommodating land. There were many young women, like Mary Ormando, that worked tirelessly on their English. They worked on their spelling, their diction, and their grammar so they would not scorned or ridiculed for sounding Italian.

MANY OF THE DISEASES that today we take for granted still ran rampant throughout the first half of the 20th century. The vaccines and treatments for these diseases simply were not known to the medical community – a community that was still trying to define itself.

In 1900, every state in the Union had some type of medical registration law with about half of all states requiring physicians to possess a medical diploma and pass an exam before they received a license to practice. However, grandfather clauses that exempted many older physicians meant that many physicians who practiced in 1918 had been poorly trained.[12]

At the start of the 20th century, the medical community was beginning to understand that there was more to the causes of sickness and disease than cleaner living conditions. Microbiology was in its formative years, and many modern vaccines and treatments were still years away. What they were beginning to understand was the link between viruses, bacteria, and disease.

This understanding should not be construed to mean that the population in general or immigrants specifically, understood these links. Living conditions were still horrendous in many immigrant communities. Overcrowded living quarters, lack of sanitary water and eating utensils, reliance on home remedies, and ignorance of the causes of disease were all factors in contributing to a lower life expectancy, and higher incidence of disease among immigrant communities. This was particularly true in communities whose immigrants came from southern Italy.

Many Sicilian immigrants maintained their beliefs that sickness and disease were caused by evil spirits or from a neighbor who gave them "mal'occhio" or the evil eye. In addition, doctors were often looked at with the same suspicion as government officials or clergy members. Together, it made for an environment ripe for the spread of disease. One of the most dreaded of these was tuberculosis.

La Grippe, as Tuberculosis was known, has been in existence throughout the course of history. It is still one of the critical issues in health care worldwide. Tuberculosis is caused by strains of mycobacteria, typically *Mycobacterium tuberculosis*. It is spread through the sneezing, coughing or spitting of an infected person. If left untreated Tuberculosis is fatal. Even today, over 50% of those who contract the disease, die regardless of when it is detected or how it is treated.

IN THE EARLY 20TH CENTURY, American women had the highest maternal mortality rate of any industrialized nation. The rate in 1934 was approximately 59 deaths per 10,000 births.[13] There were many factors contributing to the high rate of death for women giving birth.

The most significant factor was poverty. For immigrants, who often barely got by on their wages, the luxury of a hospital stay was non-existent. Society's attitudes toward childbirth also played a role. Obstetrics was in its infancy, and looked upon with contempt by many in the medical establishment. It was seen as women's work.

For the large percentage of immigrant women, mid-wives were used instead of doctors. The midwife that an Italian immigrant may have used in Sicily was much different from the one she would encounter in America.

The midwife of the early 20th century in America was not the trained medical profession that it is today. There were few rules or regulations governing who could be a midwife and virtually no training with live births. The only training that most American midwives received was an oral exam, consisting of recently memorized answers. By 1916, there were only two states with regulations governing the practice of midwifery.

Midwives were expected to repair lacerations incurred during the birthing process, "unless they were quite serious."[14] Some relied on divine intervention for assistance. "God helped her [the mother] and the birth was easy," said one midwife. Another used "old methods, but always had good luck."[15]

There was a prejudice against a male doctor assisting in a birth, to the point where a woman was made to feel shame if such assistance was rendered. Only when a woman giving birth was on the verge of death would her family consider bringing in a physician. By then, it was often too late.

Having births at home, without medical assistance led to unsanitary conditions during the birthing process. Sepsis accounted for about 40% of the maternal deaths prior to prenatal care and women giving birth at hospitals. The other 60% of the deaths were accounted for through other forms of infection, hemorrhaging, and accidents that occurred.

Soon after giving birth, mothers were expected to resume their normal household duties. If lodgers were present in the home, this meant looking after their needs in addition to their newborn child. It is no wonder that without proper medical care, or time for recovery, maternal mortality was an ongoing danger for immigrant mothers.

The Ormando family was not immune to the tragedy of maternal mortality. Mary DiLorenzo Maloney, whose story will be presented later in this narrative, died due to complications from childbirth in 1943.

DISCRIMINATION AND PREJUDICE have been a persistent part of American history. They have existed here since this country was formed. Until 1865, an entire race of people was enslaved, ceasing only with the passage of the 14th Amendment, and the ending of the Civil War.

The treatment of Native Americans, during our period of westward expansion is a shameful chapter in our history. The disenfranchisement of women voters prior to the passage of the 19th Amendment in 1920 was another form of discrimination. The list of discriminating behaviors in American history is as mindless as it is endless.

According to the Merriam-Webster Dictionary, prejudice is a "(1) preconceived judgment or opinion (2): an adverse opinion or leaning formed without just grounds or before sufficient knowledge."[16] It defines discrimination as a "prejudiced or prejudicial outlook, action, or treatment."[17] Therefore, prejudice is the adverse thought that an individual or group of individuals has regarding a person or group of people; while discrimination is those actions taken by an individual or group of individuals to express their prejudice.

One group of people who suffered from discrimination was Italian immigrants. This was particularly true for immigrants from Southern Italy. Italian immigrants were most loathed by Irish-Americans.

Though both groups were largely Roman Catholic, the Irish cursed the Italians for their religious feast days and mocked their old-world superstitions. They also loathed the Italians for taking low-paying jobs they felt were beneath an Irishman's dignity.

Italian immigrants, in particular, were thought to be prone to violence due to racially driven stereotypes. Many Americans believed that "crimes of personal violence, robbery, blackmail, and extortion [were] peculiar to the people of Italy."[18] This stereotype was especially true for Italian immigrants from Sicily.

BEING A SICILIAN IMMIGRANT in the early 20th century meant being stereotyped, ridiculed, ostracized, and discriminated against by their fellow Americans. Sicilians were thought to be sub-human, and words like "dago," "wop," and "guinea" were often used to describe them.

The word "wop" was an acronym for without papers, as sometimes Italians came looking for work without the proper immigrant paperwork. "Dago," meaning as the days goes, is derived from the notion that Italians were often hired as day laborers. Regardless of their meaning, they were derogatory and meant to humiliate.[19]

Public officials often encouraged these stereotypes. H.G. Wells stated "the arrival of Eastern Europeans, Jews and Italians would cause a huge dilution of the American people with profoundly ignorant foreign peasants."[20] Congressman Albert Johnson (R-Washington), who co-authored legislation in 1924 that restricted the immigration of Eastern and Southern Europe stated "our capacity to maintain our cherished institutions stands diluted by a stream of alien blood, with all of its misconceptions respecting the relationships of the governing power to the governed."[21]

The racist undertones of the phrase "diluted by a stream of alien blood" are eerily similar to words that Adolph Hitler would later use to describe those races he deemed unfit in Nazi Germany.

The largest mass lynching in American history was in New Orleans in 1891. The chief of police there had been murdered because he was investigating the mafia's possible links to crime in the area. Ten Italians were put on trial for the crime, and all ten were acquitted. A mob of 5,000 stormed the jail where the men were being held. They were shot and lynched. While the national press called the lynching deplorable, they also described Italians as devious anarchistic thieves bent infiltrating American society with their camorra.[22]

Many Americans believed that all Italians, and especially Sicilians, were members of the mafia, the "Black Hand," or worst of all, anarchists. The case of Sacco and Vanzetti provides an instructive lesson for understanding this stereotype.

FERDINANDO SACCO AND BARTOLOMEO VANZETTI were suspected anarchists that were convicted of a 1920 double murder committed during an armed robbery. The crime took place at a shoe factory in Braintree, Massachusetts on April 15, 1920.

The target of the robbery was the payroll of the Slater-Morris Company shoe factory. The paymaster, Frederick Parameter, was shot twice as was his security guard Alessandro Berardelli. Police suspected the robbery was the work of a local gang of Italian anarchists. Sacco and Vanzetti were soon arrested for the crime. Neither man had a police record at the time.

The two men were questioned, mostly about their politics, without any mention of why they had been arrested. There were no *Miranda Rights* in 1920, and Sacco and Vanzetti were not told that they were suspected of murder.

Their trial was held in Dedham, Massachusetts, and the prosecution's case was largely circumstantial, and circumspect – No matter. The jury found them guilty of the double murder, and the judge sentenced them to death. Throughout the trial, the prosecution mocked the defendant's halting English, and reminded the jurors that they were known anarchists. For the jury, the fact that the men were Italian and anarchists meant that they must be guilty of the crime they were accused of committing.

Though there were international protests supporting Sacco and Vanzetti, the two were executed on 23 August 1927. They met their fate largely due to their being Italian, an inability to speak English well, and political views that were considered outside the norm.

It is unfortunate that southern Italy had a long history of the presence of criminal organizations such as the *Black Hand* and the mafia. This helped lead to the stereotype that all Sicilians were robbers and hooligans. This was the ignorance of American society in the early 20th century. This stereotype exists to this day. I have been asked numerous times if any member of my family had ever been in the mafia.

The word "mafia" was never spoken in Ormando family homes. The mafia struck fear into the hearts of many Italians. For them, it was also about shame.

They were ashamed that Italians were stereotyped as being associated with a criminal organization.

In much the same way, they were mortified when Benito Mussolini became dictator in Italy and joined the Tripartite Pact with Nazi Germany and Imperial Japan. The Ormando family did not want to be associated with a megalomaniac dictator.

THE WORST ECONOMIC CALAMITY in the modern era began on 29 October 1929. The price of stocks slid to all-time lows. All sectors of the economy were hit hard by the depression, including the coal mining industry. Because oil, natural gas, and electricity were less expensive, consumers from the cities of the northeastern United States turned away from coal. Moreover, the leaders of the coal industry did themselves no favors by not looking for new markets for their product.

Coal production throughout the anthracite region declined. Mines began to close, leaving many coalminers unemployed with nowhere to turn. At 324,000 people – across all occupations - Pennsylvania had the largest number of people in the country seeking relief.[23]

Many aspects of life were affected by the Great Depression. Divorce rates dropped significantly, as there were 170,000 fewer divorces between 1930 and 1935 than would have been expected if the rates experienced in the 1920s were sustained. However, many men – unable to face their loved ones without a job – abandoned their families during the same period.

Other couples delayed getting married because they could not afford a family. This brought about the phenomenon of the "long engagement."[24]

For the Ormando family, at least one man of working age, per household, was working through most of the Depression. However, there were periods of unemployment and economic need. When they did work, it was often for less pay than they had received before the Depression. My ancestors were some of the lucky few that did not suffer through losing their homes, families, or their dignity.

The Great Depression did affect the Ormando family in other ways. The education of children in the family suffered because of the need to have more members of the household available for work. Joseph Ormando's daughters, Susan and Josephine, left school early to go to work. The both worked in the garment industry. Their brother James left school prematurely to work as a repairperson. They were not bitter later in life for having left school early, for they knew they did what they had to do to for their family.

Many children in other families left school early to help bring money into their households. It was a desperate time that called for extraordinary measures to be taken.

As welfare did not exist at the time, there was no one to turn to but one's family. Sicilian immigrants did this for centuries before coming to America. No economic calamity would break apart their families.

5 – How They Lived

There were many ways that Sicilian immigrants managed the challenges that they faced. There were benevolent societies, designed to help members cope in a crisis. Italian-language newspapers helped the immigrant keep up with the news of the day in America, and often in Italy as well. There was a variety of housing arrangements to accommodate their needs. Saloons and meeting halls provided a place for relaxation, and for transit, there was the interurban street trolley called the *Laurel Line*. Together, these varied means helped the immigrant become comfortable in their new surroundings and began the process of assimilation into their new way of life.

9 - Sam Prizzi, one of the founding members of the San Cataldo Society. Courtesy of Rosalie Prizzi

IMMIGRANTS DEVISED WAYS to cope with their social and emotional needs. To moderate the potentially devastating effects of illness, disability, or death, immigrants banded together to form benevolent societies. The first voluntary associations operated on the basic principle that members would lend one another a helping hand in time of need and take care of funeral arrangements should that be necessary.

Individuals paid dues to maintain a treasury, used to dispense small sickness or unemployment benefits. In the event of a member's death, each person in the society was assessed a larger amount to pay for burial expenses. By extending aid in times of need (and promising that someone would handle their funerals), these early self-help organizations provided immigrants with some of the same security they had known in their homeland villages and towns.[1]

Many Italians in the Wyoming Valley formed or joined benevolent societies, including the San Cataldo Society. The *San Cataldo Society* was founded in 1907 and had 75 charter members, including its first president Sam Prizzi.

At first, the society held their meetings at St. Aloysius Hall, located at 77 South Main Street in Pittston, Pennsylvania. Gaetano Leonardi, was a lifelong member of the San Cataldo Society. He would walk from his residence – first from 5 West Oak Street, and later from 225 South Main Street – to the Societies' meetings.

The organization helped to pay sick and death benefits for its members. By September 1939, the society moved to a new location at 185 South Main Street.[2] On 8 October 1939, the society held its benediction ceremony for the new building, and Sam Prizzi was one of the principal speakers that evening. The guest of honor was the mayor of Pittston, K. J. English.[3]

In 2007, the *San Cataldo Society* celebrated their 100th anniversary. Several of the fourth generation of the Ormando family attended the celebration, including Rosalie Prizzi, granddaughter of Salvatore Prizzi.

ANOTHER BENEVOLENT SOCIETY with significance to the Ormando family was the *Serradifalco Society*. Several of those who married into the Ormando family were from Serradifalco, including Angelo DiLorenzo and Michel Aquilina.

Originally, membership in the *Serradifalco Society* was restricted to men born in Serradifalco. New members had to demonstrate that they were physically able to work before membership would be granted.

They paid dues of twenty-five cents per month; this permitted members to borrow from the society in times of need, such being ill or injured and unable to work. The weekly benefit, about $5.00 was not much, but it was better than having no money at all.

If a member faked illness or injury, that could be cause for expulsion from the society. Members took their rules very seriously. Death benefits were also paid by the *Serradifalco Society*. This usually involved the wake of the deceased member being held in their home. This why, in many death announcements from the 1920s and 30s, one will often see the words "from the home" when the article refers to a wake.

Women formed auxiliary clubs and facilitated many of the religious fiestas held by the society. One of these festivals honored Mary, Mother of Sorrows. The festival would feature a statue of Mary at the head of a procession. Attendees of the procession would pin money to the statue.

These festivals provided a way for members to express their religious beliefs and helped the society raise funds. The Pittston chapter has held this festival every year since 1914. The *Serradifalco Society* still has a chapter today in Pittston, with many of its members being the great-grandchildren of the founders.

While these societies and many others served their purposes well in their formative years, their roles have evolved. Initially, most of their focus was internally focused – companionship with other Italians, helping to pay modest funeral expenses, and maintaining religious traditions.

These societies also helped bring unions to prominence in the coal industry, because the unions sought the better pay and working conditions that were supported by the benevolent societies.

Today, the remaining benevolent societies support cultural events, and support efforts to fight discrimination against Italians. They also serve as a gathering place for members to honor the memories of their ancestors who paved the way for the lives they enjoy today.

HOUSING FOR ITALIAN IMMIGRANTS consisted of a variety of arrangements. Boarding houses, rear-dwellings, many families living within the same house were all common dwellings. The lucky few owned their own homes.

The practice of several families living at one physical address was not unique to Italian immigrants. However, their reasons for doing so were their historical reliance on family, and extended family for support.

According to the 1910 United State Census, Cataldo Amico owned the residence at 18 Price Street in Pittston. This was somewhat remarkable, considering he had been in America for less than ten years, and the wages he would have made as a coalminer. Along with his wife and three of their children, Frank and Mary Ormando Agati; and Gaetano and Grace Occhipenti Ormando, were listed as renters at that same residence[4]. Cataldo Amico was also a very enterprising man.

He cultivated his own vegetable garden in his backyard. Cataldo sold the surplus that he grew to many people, including his own relatives. Cataldo also made his own wine. In the cellar of his home, the grapes were stomped by foot, and then fermented into wine. This wine was also sold to his friends and family in Pittston.

By 1930, both Gaetano and Grace Ormando passed away; Frank Agati had been murdered; and Mary Agati was now living with her children in Wyoming, Pennsylvania. Cataldo and Josephine Amico by now had seven children altogether. Their oldest child, Nellie, had been a widow once, and was now married to Michele Aquilina.

In the 1930 United States Census, Nellie and Michele were listed as renters at 18 Price Street, along with their seven children, including two from her previous marriage and three from Michele's previous marriage.[5]

A similar living arrangement could be seen at 5 West Oak Street. Joseph Ormando owned the residence at 5 West Oak Street. There, on the first floor, he lived with his wife, Grace Grifasi, and seven of their nine children. Renting the second floor was their daughter Mary, her husband Gaetano Leonardi, and their three children. Finally, renting the third floor was Joseph's daughter Grace, her husband Angelo DiLorenzo, and their five children. In all, there were three families and twenty people residing at 5 West Oak Street.[6]

A second type of residence was the rear dwelling. Often, when looking through a census from 1910 or 1920, one will find an address that looks like the following: 320R Elizabeth Street, Anywhere, USA. The "R" in the address indicates that it is a rear dwelling. These "dwellings" could be dismal places to live.

Rear dwellings could more aptly be described as single room apartments. They usually received no direct sunlight, so that they were often dark and dank. Light was needed at all hours for their occupants to see anything. They were terribly hot in the summer, and the enclosed surroundings in the winter kept any foul odors from escaping.

Perhaps for a single male, or a new couple starting out, the rear dwelling could be tolerable. It was not an arrangement one would countenance for a permanent dwelling.

The practice of living in boarding houses was quite common among Italian immigrants, especially the males. For economic point of view, this living arrangement worked well for the boarders as well as the homeowners. For the homeowners, it was a way to supplement their income derived from the salary of a coal miner. For the boarder, it was an inexpensive place to live.

> Boarders were often less concerned with sleeping arrangements than with bottom-line costs and the kinds of services available. For their part, boardinghouse operators and families who accepted lodgers wanted to ensure not only that they received proper payment but also that roomers understood what services they could expect.
> These mutual interests turned boarding into a business based on clear understandings. Men and women who operated the boardinghouse specified the services they would provide and how costs would be calculated. Boarders promised to pay their share of expenses.[7]

The arrangement also had many positive social attributes for the mostly men living in boarding houses. They were able to spend their evenings with other men that they probably knew from Italy; were able to speak a language they could understand; share information about family still living in Italy; eat food that they were familiar with; and on occasion share their musical talents with the other boarders.

WHEN THE ORMANDO FAMILY first came to the Pittston area, newspapers (written in English) were the main source of news. Radio did not come into wide use in the United States until the 1920s.

Fortunately, for the new Italian immigrant there were a many Italian language newspapers. In the early 20th Century, many of the dailies held little editorial value, and instead focused on advertising questionable medical treatments; and extremist views, some of which were considered un-American in their tone. Quite a few of these dailies failed, as immigrants became assimilated into society.

There were; however, other mainstream Italian-language newspapers that flourished. By 1922, these newspapers included the *La Stella d'Italia* in Connecticut; *Il Progresso Italo-Americano* in New York; *La Gazzetta del Massachusetts* in Boston; and the *Il Corriere del Popolo* in San Francisco. Gaetano Leonardi, read the *Il Progresso* every day, and was well versed in the news and politics of the day.

For those who could not read English, and often not speak it when the first immigrated, being able to read a newspaper in one's own language, these periodicals provided a way for immigrants to stay current on world and local events. The Italian-language newspapers also provided immigrants with a way to trace lost relatives, by publishing ads asking for information about family members. Benevolent societies also boosted their membership by regularly publishing articles about their groups' activities in the paper.

Doctors, lawyers, and bankers placed ads in the Italian language newspapers, thereby making immigrants aware of services they might otherwise not have known of. Other service providers and retailers also advertised in the Italian language newspapers, making their goods and services known to immigrants as well.

By the end of World War I, there were still 1,052 foreign language newspapers in circulation in the United States. Though most are now defunct, the foreign language newspapers clearly filled a need that would otherwise have gone unmet.

IMMIGRANT-RUN MEETING PLACES, such as coffeehouses, saloons, and billiard halls offered the mostly male clients a place to socialize with other Sicilians. It was a place where they were welcome after a hard day's work. The men often shared stories from back home, drank wine and smoked cigarettes and cigars until closing time.

Oftentimes, the patrons could be found playing some of the traditional Italian trick taking card games, such as *tresette*, *scopa*, or *briscola*. Occasionally, one might find a game of dice being played.

Games of pool were also quite popular, if the owner of the establishment could afford one. These saloons and coffeehouses filled a need, particularly for new immigrants, who often lacked organized means of socializing with others who shared their culture and language.

The benefits of these establishments notwithstanding, teetotalers and conservative religious organizations viewed them with an eye askance. In their view, the mostly poor immigrants should not have been spending the scant money they had on liquor and games of chance. Generally, the Sicilian immigrants did not spend their last dime at saloons or coffeehouses, nor did they become alcoholics.

To give a general idea of their prevalence, in 1920 there were over 90 saloons in the greater Pittston area, though only four of them appear to have catered to Sicilians. There were also many other immigrant communities in the area, such as the Irish, Poles, Lithuanians, and Germans. Of the 20 or so billiard halls in Pittston, one or two accommodated Sicilian customers.

As immigrants became assimilated into society, the need for many saloons in the greater Pittston area catering to individual cultures began to wane. Today, the saloons that exist are neighborhood bars and no longer cater only to a particular culture.

GAETANO AND MARY ORMANDO LEONARDI never drove a vehicle in their lives. Considering how close everything they needed in life was to them, there was no reason to drive. The first and second generations of the Ormando family generally made their way on foot.

The plethora of coal mines that dotted the landscape were within walking distance for the men to go to work. Neighborhoods had their own markets for the women to obtain what was needed to run the house. Churches were always within walking distance wherever one chose to worship. Since most of the family lived close together, there was no need to drive for a Sunday visit with the rest of the family.

There were however, reasons to travel to Wilkes-Barre or Scranton for official business, or a night on the town. For these purposes, and others, there was the Lackawanna and Wyoming Valley Railroad Company, better known as the Laurel Line.

The Laurel Line was an interurban streetcar, or trolley, system that was in operation from 1903 to 1952. With eighteen stops, it ran from Scranton to Wilkes-Barre. The construction of the Laurel Line drew these disparate cities closer together than they ever would have been if left to their own devices.

10 - Pittston Depot for the Laurel Line, circa 1910. Courtesy of the Luzerne County Historical Society.

A passenger boarding a streetcar in Pittston at 9:30am could be in Scranton by 9:50am. Likewise, one could leave Pittston at 9:30am and be in Wilkes-Barre by 9:45am.[8]

The Laurel Line was important to the Italian immigrant community in another way. One of the stops on the line was Rocky Glen, a large amusement park near Moosic, Pennsylvania. A highlight of every summer, when there were no summer vacations, was Italian Day at Rocky Glen. The Ormando family and other Italian families packed lunches and went for a day of socializing and listening to Italian music.

For passengers, the system was efficient and reliable. For the railroad company, it was not profitable. The Lackawanna and Wyoming Valley Railroad Company tried to bolster its profitability by transporting coal from the mines in the Wyoming Valley to transit depots.

At the transit depots, the coal would be loaded onto locomotives that carried them to the big cities of the northeastern United States. While coal was king in the Wyoming Valley, this system did help the railroad company raise the bottom-line. With the decline of coal in the 1950s, however, there was no longer any viable use of the line for freight. This left passenger service as the remaining use for the Laurel Line.

However, after World War II, ridership declined. This had much to do with the coming of the interstate highway system, the availability of automobiles, and the use of locomotive trains for passenger service. The last trolley ran on 31 December 1952.

ITALY HAS A LONG STORIED history with regard to music, so much, so that it is part of Italy's national identity. Opera, Classical instrumental music, and sacred music are all part of the fabric of this identity. Italy has provided some of the true titans of music, including Puccini, Verdi, and Vivaldi. The overwhelming contribution to music by Italians has been spectacular.

In 1896, *La Bohème* premiered in Turin, Italy.[9] Written by Giacomo Puccini, It was the first opera that was written in *verismo* (realistic) style to include all aspects of life, including the despicable. The opera is a series of vignettes that focus on the lives of two Parisian bohemians Rodolfo and Mimi. The crescendo of the opera occurs at the death of Mimi and the resulting agonies of the grieving Rodolfo. It is still one of the most frequently performed operas throughout the world.

Opera was so important to my grandparents that, even in the most challenging economic circumstances, they somehow managed to cobble together enough money to go to the opera. The San Carlo Company would perform at the Temple Theater in Scranton, Pennsylvania. The Charles L. Wagner Opera Company would perform at the Kingston High Auditorium in Kingston, Pennsylvania.

A few times, my grandparents were able to afford the trip to New York City to view opera performances at the Metropolitan Opera House. Among their precious belongings today are the librettos from many of the operas that they attended in the 1940s and 50s, including *La Boheme, Cavalleria Rusticana*, and *Il Trovatore*.

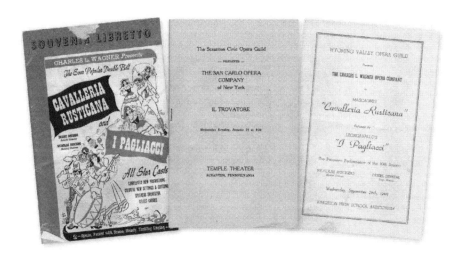

11 - Librettos from operas attended by Gaetano and Mary Ormando Leonardi

Gaetano Leonardi was such an aficionado of opera that he would listen to them on the radio faithfully every Saturday during the season, much to the dismay of his children.

Throughout the Ormando family there were, and are today, musicians and the musically inclined. Many performed at church minstrels, sang in church choirs, performed musical numbers at family gatherings, or became accomplished musicians in their own right.

6 – The Family at Home

FOR THE ORMANDO FAMILY, life at home was about tradition. Men and women had traditional roles that they were expected to follow. Children too had roles they were expected to follow. The traditions of and roles within Sicilian families were followed in America as they had been in Sicily. For the first and second generation of immigrants, this pattern held true. For the third generation of the family, though, life would be different. They would be more assimilated into American society. Women would work outside of the home, and children were expected to finish high school.

AT HOME, THE FATHER was the head and master of his house. Obedience and respect were expected from the wife and children. This male dominated culture was centuries in the making, from the time of Roman law through the unification under the leadership of Giuseppe Garibaldi.

Several factors contributed to this culture in Southern Italy. First, there was the progenitor – What belongs to the father becomes the property of the first-born son. The first-born son was expected to take his place as the man of the house when his father became too old or died.

The second factor was the relationship between the peasant population in Sicily and the church in Rome. Most Italians viewed the church with a suspicious eye, as they believed that the church was just as corrupt as were their local officials. The citizens came to rely first on the family before anything else. This eventually meant relatives as well as their immediate families.

Further contributing to this culture was the ever-changing nature of their governing officials. Peasants and farmers knew they could count on no one but themselves and their families. There were no social services, government officials, or clergy to turn to for help – there was only the family.

These circumstances led to Southern Italians generally having large families – Six or more children in a household were common. As soon as the male children were able to work, they were expected to work.

For the women, there was no expectation of property being handed down from generation to generation. If the husband's property was left to his first-born son, there were no alternative means of earning a living for the wife. There were no career paths to follow. If one was born a farmer's son or daughter that is what you would remain for the rest of your life.

In most Italian households, the men were usually eight to ten years older than their spouses were. For the first and second generations of the Ormando family, the average difference in age was 7.7 years.

The male dominance extended to the children in the family. Sons were allowed a free hand and generally could come and go as they pleased. The same could not be said for the women in Italian families.

Lucille Leonardi, daughter of Gaetano and Mary Ormando Leonardi, recalls not being allowed to go to the store, or the movies, without the accompaniment of a male relative – a cousin, and uncle, sometimes her father. To be seen with a boy without a male relative nearby would be unthinkable.

Similarly, when girls started dating, it was always in the presence of a chaperon. This was also customary in the Ormando family, as Gaetano Leonardi and Mary Ormando always had a chaperon while they were courting.

FOR THE ORMANDO WOMEN born in America, this was not a satisfactory arrangement. They wanted the freedom that they saw that other American girls had. Their fathers, though, would hear none of that. In 1936, Grace DiLorenzo (b, 1918) and her aunt Carmela Ormando (b, 1915) decided to rebel and ran off to New York, via bus, to seek fun, adventure, and most of all freedom.

Their fathers Angelo DiLorenzo and Joseph Ormando discovered their chicanery and quickly set off to find them. One must keep in mind that neither man spoke English particularly well.

They first went to the Pittston bus depot to determine where their daughters had gone. Soon thereafter, they took the next bus to New York in search of the girls.

One can only imagine the humiliation that Grace and Carmela must have felt at the sight of their fathers finding them in New York and taking them back to Pittston[1]. It is unimaginable to today's generation that two women, 18 and 21 years old, would not be allowed to go where they wanted and when they wanted to go there.

Carmela further displeased her father later that year when she announced that she was leaving home to be married. A short time later, she returned home to admit that she had not been married, and that she had left home to be free from the stifling influence of her father.

Joseph Ormando was furious and refused to allow Carmela to live in his home. This was mostly "bella figura," or saving face, for Carmela was living with the Gaetano Leonardi family at 5 West Oak Street. They lived on the second floor of the house. Joseph Ormando, his wife and their remaining children at home all lived on the first floor of 5 West Oak Street.

FOR THE WOMEN IN THE FAMILY that observed the traditional role of homemaker in the Italian family, opportunities for social interaction were considerably more limited. Some had informal "clubs" with whom they socialized. The members of these clubs were always other homemakers, or widows.

12 - "The Ladies." Grace Ormando DiLorenzo is first on the left. Mary Ormando Leonardi is fourth from the right.

Mary Ormando Leonardi and her sister Grace Ormando DiLorenzo were members of a club they called "the ladies." "The ladies" was a small group of homemakers that got together informally. Usually, they rotated between houses for their next get together. It was an important outlet for them, and gave them a way to socialize outside the home.

THERE IS A NAMING CONVENTION for Italians that has been a long-standing tradition:

- The first son is named after the paternal grandfather
- The first daughter is named after the paternal grandmother
- The second son is named after the maternal grandfather
- The second daughter is named after the maternal grandmother

This pattern held true for the second generation of the Ormando family in naming their children. One other peculiarity about this tradition is worth mentioning. If child (son or daughter) died at a young age, and another child is born of the same gender, then that child often received the same name as its deceased sibling. This happened with Gaetano Ormando's family, as well as the Agati and Amico families. The pattern was repeated in many other Sicilian immigrant families.

Sometimes a family would alter a given name to make it more American sounding. Cataldo and Josephine Ormando Amico named their first daughter Calogera. She was born in Sicily in 1898. When their first son was born seven years later in Pittston, they named him Sebastiano. He was born in Pittston in 1906, and became known as "Sam." Such was the stigma for Italian immigrants that they sometimes felt it necessary to Americanize their children's given names.

WEDDINGS WERE VERY IMPORTANT occasions in Italian families. Especially with the second generation of the Ormando family, the parents managed the event with the bride and groom having little if any involvement in the decisions.

It was expected that the oldest daughter would marry first, and was considered a misfortune if a girl was not married by the time she was twenty-three years old. If a girl was not married, she could expect to be made fun of and insulted in public.

The Old Italian saying, "an unmarried woman is like a fly without a head" gives some indication of how unmarried women were viewed in Italian culture. A girl's father and brothers would do their best to find a suitable husband.

The practice of arranged marriage was particularly strong in Southern Italy. Arranged marriage was practiced with the second generation of the Ormando family, including Joseph Ormando and Grace Grifasi. Once a marriage had been arranged, the joyful occasion of the wedding would be anticipated by everyone in the family.

It was considered bad luck to marry during May or August, and often forbidden during Lent. According to the Catholic Church, Lent was a time of self-sacrifice and weddings were considered indulgent during the Lenten season. The tradition of a diamond engagement ring dates to medieval times when the people believed that diamonds came from the flames of love.

13 - Tony Ormando and Mollie DePascale's wedding party, 10 September 1937
Courtesy of Sylvia Ormando

The best day of the week to marry on was a Sunday. Modern tradition holds that the groom should not see his bride on the day of the wedding before the ceremony.

By contrast, in Italy tradition held that the bride and groom should walk to the church together. Grooms often carried a piece of iron ore in their pockets to ward off evil spirits. The bride was not to wear any gold to her wedding, lest she bring bad luck to the marriage.

At the reception, guests toasted the bride and groom with the traditional "per cent'anni," meaning "for one hundred years!" Kissing the bride is another tradition that began in Italy. It was a way for the groom to show affection to his new bride in front of their guests.

In the first and second generation of the Ormando family, women tended to marry much earlier than is considered appropriate today. Several were married by the time they were 14, and most of those had their first child by the age of 15.

SICILIAN IMMIGRANT FAMILIES tended to look out for one another, and the Ormando family was no exception. There were many instances two or more families shared the same dwelling. In reviewing the family history and the United States Censuses in 1910, 1920 and 1930 patterns emerged.

When the family first immigrated to America, those that arrived first accommodated those who followed them to America. These were certainly not the best of circumstances for raising one's family, or having any privacy at all.

Still, it was an accepted practice and economically essential to immigrant families, whose fathers worked in the coalmines, and whose mothers – for the most part – were expected to stay at home, take care of the children, make meals, and keep the house in working order.

By 1920, multiple families in one dwelling occurred because a child was married with children of their own. Most of the men in the Ormando family in 1920 were miners, and buying one's own home was not a luxury a man with a new family could afford.

By 1930, multiple families living in the same home was owed to the Great Depression. Those that were able to keep their homes made room for those who had fallen on hard times. Combing through the 1930 Census, there are many other examples – in Luzerne County alone – of multiple families sharing dwellings with the same physical address.

ONE OF THE ORMANDO FAMILY traditions was to have family reunions at one of the many parks in either Luzerne or Lackawanna County. There were many to choose from – Rocky Glenn (whose picnic grounds were part of a larger amusement park), Sans Souci, Fernbrook, and Fanti's Park.

They were just a few of the parks that were a train, bus, or car ride away. Fanti's Park was the favorite gathering place for the Ormando family reunions. As it happened, Fanti's Park was an Italian immigrant success story.

Sinibaldo Fanti was born 5 July 1884 in Pistoia, Italy. He immigrated to America on the vessel *Sempione*, arriving 9 January 1900 at Ellis Island in New York.[2] Together with his wife, Maria Neinna, they made their way to Swoyersville, Pennsylvania.

There they lived at 383 Shoemaker Street, while Sinibaldo worked as a grocery merchant. Sinibaldo and Marie would have four children including Devilio, Eldia, Jennie, and Rudolph.[3]

By the late 1930s, he had saved enough money to buy what was then Cummins' Pond, near the Township of Franklin, Pennsylvania. Sinibaldo established his family's residence there at #3 Dallas Road in Franklin Township, Luzerne County, Pennsylvania.

In 1937, he opened Fanti's Park and pavilion on the site of the former Cummins' Pond. He operated the park until his death on 1 October 1946.[4] Through the mid-1960s, families, clubs, organizations, churches, and the Ormando family all held picnic gatherings at Fanti's Park.

O Great St. Rocco, deliver us, we beseech you, from contagious diseases, and the contagion of sin. Obtain, for us, a purity of heart, which will assist us to make good use of health, and to bear sufferings with patience. Teach us to follow your example in the practice of penance and charity, so that we may, one day enjoy the happiness of being with Christ, Our Savior, in Heaven. Amen. – Prayer to Saint Rocco

14 - Saint Rocco's Church, circa 1927. Courtesy of The Luzerne County Historical Society

THE BEAUTIFUL CHURCH at 62 West Oak Street is no longer home to a congregation. By 2011, the Scranton Diocese found that it had too few priests to serve a declining number of parishioners across too many parishes. Because of this, after 90 years of service to the community, Saint Rocco's Italian Catholic Church in Pittston closed in 2012.

The church was built and founded by members of the Saint Rocco's Society of Pittston in 1920. From that time, until its closing, it was the scene of many baptisms, marriages, and funerals for five generations of the Ormando family.

When visiting the Wyoming Valley, one soon notices the many churches the dot the landscape. With regard to Roman Catholic Churches, sometimes there are two or three churches in a single town.

One of the reasons Saint Rocco's church was built, specifically for Sicilians, was they were not welcome at other Italian Catholic churches. Even within the Italian community, Sicilians suffered from a cultural bigotry.

My parents were married at Saint Rocco's, I was baptized at Saint Rocco's church, and my grandparents' funerals were held there as well. The church was important to many members of the Ormando family.

The parishioners of Saint Rocco's church were exceptionally devoted to the church and its patron saint, Saint Rocco. To understand their devotion, one must understand the life, martyrdom, and legacy of Saint Rocco.

SAINT ROCCO IS ONE OF ITALY'S most revered saints, prayed to and celebrated for protection from disease and sin. He was born in 1340 A.D. to noble parents in Montpelier, France. Even as a young boy, he was devoted to God and the Blessed Mother. While still a young boy, his parents died, leaving him an orphan in the care of an uncle, the Duke of Montpelier.

Rocco gave away all of his worldly wealth and took a vow of poverty. While on a pilgrimage to Rome, he stopped in many villages where plague was ravaging their inhabitants to pray and heal with the sign of the cross. Village after village, Rocco repeated his healing prayers, and the plague left those villages where he performed his miracles – in Cesena, Mantua, Modena, and Parma.

Finally, Rocco became of victim of the plague, as festering sore on his leg would attest. Banished from the town, he sought refuge in a cave. A nobleman found him, and took him to his castle where Rocco was healed.

Upon his return to France, he was thrown in jail as a spy. His own people did not recognize Rocco; being so weak from years of disease, they were suspicious of any newcomer who might bring plague.

For five years, he languished in prison until 16 August 1378 when a guard entered Rocco's cell saw him near death. A blue light was emanating from his body. Upon hearing of this, the governor of the town went to the prison and demanded to know Rocco's identity. Rocco told him "I am your nephew, Rocco."

When Rocco was born, he bore a birthmark in the shape of a cross. This birthmark was used to identify the now near-death Rocco. The governor and the people from the town there at the prison believed in the divine actions of St. Rocco.

Shortly after Rocco's death Sicily experienced a cholera epidemic; the people prayed to Saint Rocco for protection from the epidemic that plagued them. Since that time, Sicilians have prayed to Saint Rocco for protection against sickness and disease. When they immigrated to America, they brought their devotion to Saint Rocco with them.

Every year from 1920 through 2012, the parishioners of Saint Rocco's church in Pittston held a procession in honor of Saint Rocco. During the procession, members of the Saint Rocco Society would hoist the statue of Saint Rocco from the church and carry him through their section of the town. All along the way, devotees would pin money on his robe and offer prayers to Saint Rocco to protect them from disease and sin.

Today, the former parishioners of Saint Rocco's parish must find another church in which to worship. Parishioners were encouraged to attend Our Lady of Mount Carmel church, but many resented that suggestion. They were resentful because their ancestors had not been welcome there more than 90 years ago – before Saint Rocco's Church had been built.

7 - Biographical Vignettes

Nellie Amico

15 - The Amico family, from left – Nellie, Josephine, Grace, Cataldo, Tony, and Sam. Circa 1912. Courtesy of Vince Aquilina

Calogera "Nellie" Amico was born 22 September 1898 in San Cataldo, Sicily to Cataldo and Josephine (Ormando) Amico.[1] She grew up living at 18 Price Street in Pittston, Pennsylvania with her parents, Sister Grace, and Brothers Sam and Tony.[2]

On 21 September 1913, she married Cataldo Giannone, one day shy of her 15th birthday.[3] Cataldo was born 23 Oct 1886 in San Cataldo, Sicily to Salvatore and Rosaria (Calabrese) Giannone.[4] He came to America aboard the *San Giorgio* on 24 January 1910.[5] Cataldo made his way to Pittston to work as a coalminer.

16 - Cataldo and Nellie Giannone with their son, Sam, circa 1916. Courtesy of Vince Aquilina

Nellie and Cataldo's first child, Samuel John, was born on 5 December 1915 and their second child, Rosaria Sadie came along two and one-half years later on 4 March 1918.

On 15 September 1919, Cataldo died, from injuries he received in a coal mining accident.[6][7] Cataldo was only 29 years old. Death came early for many immigrant families, and sometimes often as well.

Following the death of her husband, 21-year-old Nellie lived in the home of her mother and father at 18 Price Street. It could have been a crushing blow for Nellie. Fortunately, Cataldo made some wise investments and left Nellie with a decent sum of money.

Her mother, Josephine, would act as her banker and held the money for Nellie. After all, she was only 21 years old when she became a first-time widow. Life would take a turn for the better, when Nellie met Michele Aquilina.

Michele Aquilina[8] was born on 19 March 1888 in Serradifalco to Calogero and Angela (Bruccheri) Aquilina.[9] When he was 19 years old, Michele married Catalda Geraci on 8 June 1907 in Serradifalco.[10] Catalda was born 12 March 1890 to Salvatore and Maria Anna Natale in Serradifalco, Sicily.[11] Together, they would have the following three children – all born in Serradifalco:

- Cologero (Charles) – 11 March 1908
- Angelina – 11 September 1909, and
- Marianna (Mary) – 13 February 1913

Michele came to America on 20 June 1913 through Philadelphia, Pennsylvania aboard the vessel *America*, and found his way to Pittston[12]. While trying to earn enough money to bring the rest of his family to Pittston, Catalda died on 18 November 1918.[13]

Michele and Nellie would marry on 24 November 1923 at St. Rocco's Church in Pittston.[14] The average yearly income in 1923 was $1,066, though it is doubtful that Michele earned that much as a blue-collar worker.

17 - Nellie and Michele Aquilina, circa 1924.
Courtesy of Vince Aquilina

Michele's children with Catalda came to America to join their father on 9 May 1924 on board the *Giuseppe Verdi*.[15] Together, Nellie, and Michele would have five children of their own:

- Cataldo – Born 28 January 1925
- Josephine – Born 29 Oct 1926
- Anthony – Born 3 January 1929
- Joseph – Born July 1932
- Vincent – Born September 1936

Although they were a large family, Michele and Nellie always told their children that there were no stepchildren, stepbrothers, or stepsisters. They were all part of the same family. By late 1939, the house at 18 Price Street was bustling with seven members of the Cataldo Amico family along with eight from the Aquilina family residing there.

On 18 January 1940, Michele Aquilina died of pneumonia.[16] It was a cold, windswept day when Michele Aquilina was buried on a hillside in St. John's Cemetery.[17] He was only 51 years old.

In time, Nellie became the matriarch of the larger Amico family. Family members would often ask Nellie for advice and look to her for comfort in troubled times. Nellie went onto live for another 45 years, passing away 15 August 1985 at the age of 87.[18]

18 - Michele Aquilina's headstone in St. John's Cemetery

19 - Nellie Amico's headstone in Denison Cemetery

Angelo Occhipenti

Angelo Occhipenti was born in Serradifalco, Sicily on 15 March 1898 to Salvatore and Francesca (Napolitano) Occhipenti.[19] On 1 June 1903, Francesca and her four children – Maria, Rosa, Antonio, and Angelo - arrived at Ellis Island aboard the vessel *Bolivia*.[20] Their destination was Pittston, where Salvatore had established residence. It was in Pittston that Angelo would eventually meet Anna Prizzi.

Although Angelo Occhipenti shared the same last name as the matriarch of the Ormando family, Grace Occhipenti, there appears to be no direct relation to the two people. If there is a relation, they are likely distant relatives.

Ann Prizzi was born 15 August 1904 in Pittston, Pennsylvania to Salvatore and Lucy Ormando Prizzi. Anna would travel back to Sicily with her mother and brother Anthony in 1905. They returned to America on 21 June 1909 aboard the vessel *Tomaso Di Savoia*.[21] Accompanying them on this journey was Lucy's son, Ross, who was born in San Cataldo in 1906.

Angelo Occhipenti and Anna Prizzi were married in Pittston at St. Rocco's Church on 10 August 1919.[22] In the ensuing years, he and Anna had two children – Frances (1920 – 1968) and Lucille (1923 – 2007).

20 - Angelo Occhipenti and his daughter Frances.

Angelo's usual occupation was a coal miner, and on 4 November 1940, he was injured while working at the Jermyn Green Coal Company.[23] The overcrowded working conditions he found himself in may have contributed to his contracting Tuberculosis. Angelo was likely symptomatic long before the disease laid waste to him.

At first, the symptoms probably resembled a cold or flu, with sneezing and perhaps a cough. Gradually though, the cough would grow violent to the point of spitting up blood. At this stage, Angelo was most likely suffering from night sweats and a noted loss of weight. The loss of weight is why the afflicted person was called *consumptive*.

On 19 January 1946, Angelo was admitted to the White Haven Sanatorium in White Haven, Pennsylvania. "The origins of White Haven Center can be traced to August 1901 when a tuberculosis sanatorium was established on 215 acres of farmland in the Blue Mountains of Pennsylvania. Since tuberculosis is caused by various strains of mycobacteria and most common among the urban poor, the best treatment was considered isolation of the patient at rural sanitaria. White Haven offered an ideal setting due to its clean air and rural surroundings."[24]

Though the White Haven Sanatorium was well noted for its results, sadly Angelo would not be one of their success stories. Angelo Occhipenti died from Tuberculosis on 30 January 1946 at the age of 47. He is buried alongside Anna at the Dennison Cemetery in Swoyersville, Pennsylvania.

21 - Angelo Occhipenti's headstone in Denison Cemetery

22 - Anna Prizzi's headstone also in Denison Cemetery

Stephen Bellanca

23 - Stephen Bellanca and his mother, Rose Ormando Bellanca

Stephen Bellanca was born 21 Oct 1918 to Sam and Rose Ormando Bellanca in Pittston, Pennsylvania. He was the third of five children in his family, including Joseph (1914 – 1994), Anthony (1916 – 1994), Connie, and Samuel.

As fate would have it, by the time he finished high school and was ready to work, the United States was hit with the Great Depression. For several years during the late 1930s, he was one of many who were unemployed.

When jobs became available, the coal industry had employment. Stephen worked at several local collieries, while working to become an insurance agent. He did not mean to make a career of working in the coalmines.

Stephen enlisted in the United States Army on 17 May 1945. After induction and basic training, he joined the 14th Infantry Regiment as part of the occupying force in Germany. The regiment he joined had played an active role in the defeat of Nazi Germany.

The 14th Infantry Regiment departed for France in January 1945, where it would fight as part of the 71st Division of the U.S. Army. The 14th Infantry landed at Le Harve, France and drove more than 300 miles across France toward the Siegfried Line. There, they took part in breaking through Nazi Germany's defenses.

On May 5, 1945, upon reaching the Ens River, Austria, the 14th Infantry was ordered stay at its present position. With the ceasing of hostilities on May 9, the 14th

Infantry was responsible for the processing of many thousands of prisoners of war, and persons displaced by the war.

Shortly after VE Day, the 14th Infantry was relieved of its attachment to the 71st Division, and given an assignment as part of the occupying force in Germany. The 14th Infantry Regiment was deactivated on 1 September 1946.

On 1 September 1946, the 14th Infantry Regiment, for the fourth time in its long history, was deactivated. After returning stateside, Stephen was honorably discharged on 22 October 1946.

For service to his country, Stephen was awarded the World War II Victory Medal. This award was given to any soldier that served on active duty between 7 December 1941 and 31 December 1946, regardless of where that person served.

Stephen settled back into civilian life when he was discharged on 22 October 1946. About five weeks later, on 30 November 1946, Stephen married Nellie DeFrancesco.[25]

Nellie was born in 1923 to Colegro "Charles" and Mary (Lovecchio) DeFrancesco. Nellie was the fifth of seven siblings in her family including Pauline, Concetta, Angeline, Josephine, Mary, Angelo, and Louise. The family lived at 75 East Oak Street, in Pittston, Pennsylvania.

Following their marriage, Stephen and Nellie they lived at 54 East Railroad Street before moving to the Laflin section of Exeter, Pennsylvania. Stephen became an agent for the Prudential Insurance Company. In 1953, he received an award from the Prudential Insurance Company for writing $175,000 in new insurance policies that year.[26]

Nellie was a passionate supporter of the American Heart Association, in part because her father died of a heart attack on 25 May 1935. For a time, she was the co-chair of the Women's Division of Greater Pittston Heart Fund.[27]

Tragedy would strike the Bellanca family on 23 April 1958. While crossing the street near their home, Nellie was struck by a car, pulled under its wheels, and dragged approximately forty feet. Though Stephen was present at the scene, he did not witness the accident.

Nellie was taken to Pittston Hospital, but pronounced dead on arrival by the Deputy Coroner, Rufus Bierly. There were witnesses to the accident, and the driver stayed at the scene following the accident.

Ultimately, no charges were filed against the young man who was driving the car that hit Nellie. Tragically, she was in the wrong place at the worst possible time.[28]

Somehow, Stephen carried on with his life. Following his career at Prudential, he owned and operated his own business, Steve's Deli, in Wyoming, Pennsylvania for twenty years. He did marry once after the death of his beloved Nellie. Sadly, that marriage ended in divorce.

Stephen passed away at age 79 on 30 September 1998.[29] He and Nellie are buried near each other in Mount Olivet Cemetery, Kingston Township, Pennsylvania.

24 - Nellie Bellanca's Cemetery Monument   25- Stephen Bellanca's Cemetery Marker

Ross Prizzi

26 - Rosario "Ross" Calogero Prizzi

Rosario "Ross" Calogero Prizzi was born 24 Sep 1906 in San Cataldo to Sam and Lucy (Ormando) Prizzi. He immigrated to the United States on 21 July 1909 aboard the vessel *Tomaso Di Savoia*, along with his brother Anthony, his sister Anna, and his mother Lucy.[30]

The Prizzi family first lived at 107 South Main Street in Pittston. Living with them at the time were Sam's brother, Joseph, and his wife Mary.

The Prizzi family then moved to 22 Price Street, next door to the Cataldo Amico family. By 1930, they had established their family residence at 61 West Railroad Street, also in Pittston.

Ross worked his way first through school and then college at Penn State University's University Park Campus. Ross was one of the first males in the Ormando family to escape working in the coalmines, though he did work for several local mine offices. He also worked at several areas banks. It was while working as a bank employee in Duryea, Ross would meet the love of his life, Elizabeth Biscontini.

Elizabeth was born on 4 December 1905 in Old Forge, Pennsylvania to Giulio and Annetta (Rosi) Biscontini. Along with her parents, brother Hercules (John), and sister Nathalie, she lived at 1209 Main Street.

Ross and Elizabeth were married on 7 November 1934 at St. Mary's Church by the Reverend Lavezzari in Old Forge, Pennsylvania.[31] They had two daughters, Lucille and Rosalie.

Professionally, Ross worked at the Daystrom Instrument Division of Daystrom, Inc. in Archbald, Pennsylvania as an electrical engineer. Daystrom designed and manufactured precision electronic components for the United States military, including electronic gunfire control units.

By all accounts, Ross had a successful career. Engineering, though, is what he did. Being a musician is what he was, and how he saw himself. On his marriage license, he listed his occupation as musician, and what a talented musician he was.

In the late 1930s and 40s he played in many dance bands throughout the Wyoming Valley. One of these bands was Russ Andolora's Orchestra and they played Big Band Dance Music. Mr. Andolora was also Godfather to Ross' daughter Rosalie when she was baptized.

Russ Andolora and his Orchestra were well-known and played dance and concert halls throughout the Wyoming Valley. Venues they played at included Mickey's Gardens in Larksville; the Hotel Sterling in Wilkes-Barre; Sans Souci Park; and Rocky Glen. The 10-piece orchestra was always in demand, and one had only to look in the local Sunday newspaper to see where Andolora and his Orchestra would be playing next.

Ross played the double bass, and he was known as the best bass player in the Wyoming Valley. He also gave music lessons to many young men who aspired to play strings. He and his wife Elizabeth also played the violin.

In his spare time, Ross was also well known for being a master tomato grower. He and his family would annually can over 100 jars of tomatoes. His daughter Rosalie fondly remembered that her father also loved opera. He would order VHS operas and the family would watch them on Sundays. In this way, he and Elizabeth passed along their lifelong love of music to their children. Lucille and Rosalie both learned and became accomplished pianists.

By the late 1950s, Ross was playing the double bass in the Scranton Philharmonic Orchestra.[32] He continued playing with them for the next twenty years. In 1984, he was honored as a 50-year member of the American Federation of Musicians, Local 140.

Ross passed away 14 May 1996 at the age of 89.[33][34] He was followed by Elizabeth two months later on 31 July.[35] They were buried together in Denison Cemetery in Swoyersville, Pennsylvania.

Tony Amico

27 - The Amico brothers, from left Louis, Tony, Joseph, Sam (seated), and Matthew. Courtesy of Vince Aquilina

Many of us have our brushes with fame, and usually they are fleeting at best. Others not only meet famous people, they sometimes work for them. Such was the case for Tony Amico.

Anthony "Tony" Amico was born on 3 January 1911 to Cataldo and Josephine (Ormando) Amico[36]. He was born two years to the day after his sister Grace. He grew up in Pittston, living at 18 Price Street with his family including four brothers and two sisters.

By the time he was 24 years old, he knew that he wanted more than what a life in Pittston would hold in store for him. Having worked as a waiter in several area restaurants, he figured that he could land a similar job elsewhere.

He ended up landing a job as the headwaiter at the Club Miami in Newark, New Jersey in 1935. At about the same time, a young comic started working the club as the master of ceremonies who would one day become world famous. His name was Jackie Gleason.

The two men struck up a friendship, and since they were both single, decided to share an apartment. They enjoyed one another's company and could share expenses with the few dollars they were earning at the time. Tony believed in Jackie's ability as a comic, and told anyone who would listen "that kid's going to the top."[37] In that assessment, Tony was correct.

Tony Amico served his country twice. He enlisted in the U.S. Army on 31 Aug 1942. During World War II, he fought in Burmese theater. On 27 Oct 1950, he enlisted for another tour of duty, this time in Korea.

While in Korea, Tony saw frontline action at Pork Chop Hill and at the Battle of Triangle Hill. The Battle of Triangle Hill was fought October – November 1952, and was one of the bloodiest battles of the Korean War. Although the American forces suffered 1,567 casualties, the Chinese forces had 11,500 casualties. In a cruel irony, neither side gained any ground during the month-long battle.

Tony had served his country well, and Jackie was waiting for him when he returned stateside.

28 - Tony Amico during on of his two tours of duty with the U.S. Army. Courtesy of Vince Aquilina.

Over the years, Tony became Gleason's confidant, chauffer, and valet – in essence his manservant. Fortunately, Tony's personality was such that it never affected their friendship. Jackie Gleason paid tribute to his friend in an episode of his hit series *The Honeymooners*.

In the episode *Brother Ralph*, Alice Kramden takes a job as a secretary because Ralph has been laid off from his $62 a week job as a bus driver.[38]

Ralph flies into a jealous rage when he finds out that Alice is the only woman in an office with five other men – George, Frank, Pete, Bill, and her boss Tony Amico. Because of an office rule against hiring married women, Alice tells Ralph that she told her boss that she is single – and that Ralph is her brother.

Her boss comes to their apartment to pick up Alice to finish some paperwork, and Ralph's jealous charades make Tony wonder to Alice what is going on with her "brother" Ralph. Eventually, Ralph gets his job back, and sends "Tony Amico" on his way.

When Jackie Gleason married for the first time, in 1936, Tony Amico was his best man. Jackie always had a room for Tony in every New York apartment that he lived in. When Jackie later bought his dream house, Tony had his own room in the house.

The two friends finally parted ways in 1960. Tony always had fond memories of Jackie and the feeling was mutual. Following his time with Jackie Gleason, Tony lived in Geneva, New York.

According to an article by Bud Hughey, published in the *Geneva Times* in 1962 "Tony went to visit a sister and stayed with her a while. Then he made tentative arrangements for a job in Binghamton and left for that city. But, since he was in no rush, he decided to include a side-trip to Geneva to visit his old Pittston buddy Joe Sacone. He did a little over a year ago, and he never did make it to Binghamton."[39] Tony lived in Geneva, New York for the next 20 years before he passed away on 24 Jan 1982 at the age of 71.[40] He is buried in the Amico family plot in Denison Cemetery in Swoyersville, Pennsylvania.

Concetto "Frank" Agati

29 - Concetto "Frank" Agati

Concetto "Frank" Agati was born to Antonino Agati and Lucia DiSilvestro in San Cataldo on 11 June 1888.[41] In addition to Concetto, the Agati family included four other children: Rosaria, born 1883; Fortunata, born in 1885; Rosa, born in 1891; and Carmelo, born in 1894.

Frank Agati first came to America on 24 March 1907 on the vessel *Sofia Hohenberg*.[42] His brother Carmelo came to America on 26 June 1912 aboard the *Duca D Aosta*.[43] His intended destination was Pittston, Pennsylvania. There are no further records of him being in America, so it is possible that he returned to Sicily. There are no records that indicate that any of Frank's other siblings ever came to the United States.

Frank Agati married Maria Ormando on 6 February 1910.[44] It is likely that they knew each other in San Cataldo, and that this was an arranged marriage, especially since Maria was barely 15 years old at the time of their marriage.

Maria Ormando, the fourth daughter of Gaetano Ormando and Grace Occhipenti was born in San Cataldo on 8 June 1895.[45] During the period from 1910 – 1926, Frank and Mary had eight children. Their first son Antonino died when he was only 2 ½ years old on 27 March 1914.[46]

In July 1915, Agati, along with several associates became a founding member of Italian Political Club of Pittston. The stated purpose of the club was to discuss politics, political history, and to assist Italian immigrants in learning English.[47]

Frank returned to Italy several times to visit with family, until finally returning for good on 14 April 1922.[48] On all official documents to this point, Frank listed his occupation as "stone mason." By 1926, he identified himself as a "union organizer," and here is where his story takes a tragic turn.

To understand Frank's demise, one must understand the culture of violence that permeated the unionizing of coal miners in Pennsylvania.

> Coal miners were demanding better working conditions, better pay, and more fairness in general from the coal companies. The coal companies, in turn, wanted to pay as little for as much work as possible from the miners. This battle was never fought more fiercely that it was in the Pittston area in the 1920s. Added to this mix was the mafia, whose presence insured that the situation would turn into an explosive powder keg of violence.[49]

On 8 July 1923, Rinaldo Cappellini became president of the UMW, District 1 in Pittston. Rinaldo Cappellini hated the mine owners. He never forgave or forgot how shabbily he was treated by them after losing his right arm in a mining accident. After disappearing from public life for two years, he had returned wanting to avenge his wrongful treatment.

Cappellini was a popular leader amongst his followers for the tough stances he took against the mine owners. He was also reported to have ties to the mafia.

At about the same time that Cappellini became president of the United Mine Workers, District 1 Frank Agati became his principle bodyguard. Agati had also become a silent partner in the Volpe Coal Company –a conflict of interest given his status as "union organizer."

By the end of 1927, an anti-Cappellini faction had emerged in the UMW. That faction, led by international union board member Alex Campbell, was able in January 1928 to take control of [United Mine Workers Union] Local 1703, which worked Number 6 Colliery of the Pennsylvania Coal Company. Number 6, located in Pittston, was one of the operations shut down as coal companies worked to reduce the anthracite supply. The entrenched Cappellini administration sought to eliminate Campbell and his key men while reincorporating the members of his faction into the union. The conflict between the two sides resulted in a number of house bombings and murders.

Three Campbell men – Local 1703 President Samuel Bonita, Steve Mendola and Adam Moleski – visited union headquarters in Wilkes-Barre to meet with UMW district board member August Lippi. Bonita wanted Lippi's assistance in arranging negotiations to reopen Number 6 Colliery. Frank Agati interrupted the meeting. He and Bonita exchanged angry words and then gunshots. Agati fell mortally wounded.[50]

Frank died from the wounds he received during the shooting on 16 February 1928.[51] Ironically, the men who killed Frank Agati may have intended to murder Agati's boss, Rinaldo Cappellini. Unfortunately, for Frank, Cappellini was in Hazelton, Pennsylvania on the day of the murder.[52]

In Pittston, Agati was given a hero's funeral and burial on 22 February 1928. The Wilkes-Barre Times Leader described the scene.

One hundred and twenty-one automobiles conveyed the funeral cortege from the Agati home, 850 West Eight Street, West Wyoming, to Saint Rocco's Italian church at Pittston and later to St. John's cemetery in Pittston. Eleven of the automobiles carried floral tokens valued at $3,100 each and said to have been the most beautiful ever seen in this section.[53]

Shortly after Frank Agati was murdered, reprisal murders began in the Pittston area. Sam Grecio was murdered as he and his wife were walking to church. The three bullet wounds to his head were seen as retaliation for the Agati murder.

Soon thereafter, Joseph Cicero – a friend of Agati's – was murdered. His throat had been slashed, and again the police feared more retaliatory murders were in store for the Pittston area.

On 14 April 1928, Sam Bonita was found guilty of manslaughter for the killing of Frank Agati. Along with their verdict, the jury recommended mercy for the now convicted Bonita.[54] He was sentenced to six years in prison. Sometimes, there is no justice. The case of Frank Agati is one where justice was not well served.

Whatever Frank Agati may have done in life, he certainly did not deserve to be murdered for it. His wife did not deserve to be a widow at 33 years of age. Lastly, his children did not deserve to grow up without a father.

Mary DiLorenzo

30 - Mary DiLorenzo, circa 1936

Mary DiLorenzo was born on 24 September 1917 to Angelo and Grace (Ormando) DiLorenzo in Pittston, Pennsylvania. Growing up, Mary lived at her parent's home with her five siblings: Sisters Grace, Rose, and Frances; and her brothers James and Joseph. She was surrounded with people who loved her. The same could not be said for Bill Maloney, who would one day become Mary's husband.

William "Bill" Maloney was born 27 February 1911 to William and Mary Donnelly Maloney in New York City. Bill's mother died on 6 February 1913, leaving Bill without a mother at two years of age.[55] Shortly thereafter, the family relocated to the Pittston area.

His older sister, Marie S. Maloney, contracted Scarlet Fever and died on 3 January 1919.[56] Bill's father subsequently left for New York City, never to return to Pittston. By 1920, Bill was being raised in the home of his grandfather, Patrick Maloney, living at 138 Vine Street in Pittston.[57]

During the Great Depression, Mary occasionally found work in the garment industry. Finding employment during the Depression was especially difficult for women. When they did work, their pay was typically 45% less than did their male counterparts. For garment workers like Mary, this meant an average of $6 a week, or 14 cents per hour. Bill found work as a baker during the Depression, and managed to keep steady work through most of those difficult years.

Mary DiLorenzo and Bill Maloney were married 16 June 1939 in Pittston, Pennsylvania.[58] They lived at 52 Tompkins Street in Pittston following their wedding.

31 - Bill Maloney and Mary DiLorenzo on their wedding day, 16 June 1939

Mary wanted to have children, but Bill – who had already experienced the tragedy in his own life due to his mother dying young – was wary of having children. Mary became pregnant in the winter of 1942-43, and gave birth to Mary Grace in September 1943. Since the birth occurred at home with the assistance of a mid-wife, the conditions were less than sterile.

Shortly after returning home, Mary became ill. On 25 October 1943, Mary was admitted to a homeopathic hospital in Wilkes-Barre, Pennsylvania. The Sicilian disdain for the medical community may have hastened Mary's demise. On 29 October 1943, Mary Maloney died due to glomerular nephritis, and acute endocarditis.

Glomerular nephritis is "a type of kidney disease in which the part of your kidneys that helps filter waste and fluids from the blood is damaged."[59] The primary causes of this condition are inherent in the kidneys. However, secondary causes can be bacterial infections. If left untreated, renal failure will occur.

Standard treatment includes "blood pressure medications to control high blood pressure, most commonly angiotensin-converting enzyme inhibitors and angiotensin receptor blockers; and Corticosteroids."[60] Neither of these treatments would have been available through a homeopathic hospital.

Mary died when she was 26 years old, leaving a child barely one month old, and Bill Maloney – now a single father – who had just received his draft notice from the United States Navy. Though Bill asked for a deferment, based on being a single father of an infant, the Navy insisted that he report for enlistment on 22 December 1943.

Fortunately, Mary's sister Rose agreed to look after the little girl while Bill went off to war. While in the military, he served in the Navy as a Baker, Second Class in the Pacific Theater. Bill was gone for almost two years, when he was honorably discharged on 4 December 1945.[61]

While Bill was serving his country in the Navy, Rosie came to love Mary Grace as she would her own daughter. The story ends when Bill and Rose Mary DiLorenzo married in January 1946.[62] It is a story of self-sacrifice and placing the needs of a small child ahead of one's own needs.

Sadly, Mary's death was not the only tragedy to visit the DiLorenzo family during this time. Her sister Grace DiLorenzo died at the age of 23 on 23 January 1942 from acute bacterial endocarditis, and pulmonary embolism. The underlying cause was a strep throat that went untreated. Penicillin would likely have saved her life. However, it was not available to the public until 1945.

Mary's grandmother, Grace Grifasi Ormando, died from a heart attack on 19 March 1942. She was 56 years old. Finally, Mary's father, Angelo DiLorenzo, passed away later that same year on 9 November 1942 from a heart attack at the age of 48.[63] By the end of 1943, Grace Ormando DiLorenzo had lost her mother, two daughters, and her husband in less than two years. It was a sad, mournful time for the family.

32 - DiLorenzo family monument in Saint Rocco's Cemetery

Catal Ormando

33 - Catal Ormando, circa 1943

Catal James Ormando was born in San Cataldo, Sicily on 26 February 1913.[64] He was the fourth of nine children born to Joseph and Grace Ormando, and would be the last born in Sicily. Catal was barely a year old when he came to America on 11 June 1914 aboard the *Sant' Anna*, along with his brother Anthony and sisters Grace and Mary – eight, twelve and ten years old respectively. Together, they made their way to the Ormando home at 5 West Oak Street in Pittston, Pennsylvania.

Catal, or "Ky" as known by his family, made it through the tenth grade before having to leave school in order to work to support the family. He found work as a mechanic at several automobile dealerships in town. In time, he would become a master mechanic.

It was during this time that he met Rose Keating, who was working as a bookkeeper. Rose Keating was born to John J. and Mary Devers Keating on 2 March 1907 in Pittston, Pennsylvania.[65] Rose was the youngest of eight siblings.

On 12 April 1934, at the age of 21, Catal and Rose were married.[66] They lived with her parents at 542 Broad Street in Pittston. Though the couple had two children together, their marriage did not remain a happy one.

By the time the 1940 Census was taken, Catal was listed a boarder in Wilkes-Barre, living with the Peter and Miriam Carroll family.[67] He also listed himself as single. He had also met the woman who would become his second wife, Anna Kerchanin.

Anna was born 20 December 1916 to Michael and Mary Onesko Kerchanin in Wilkes-Barre, Pennsylvania. Anna was the second oldest of six girls in her family. She also had a brother, Michael.

On 19 December 1942, Catal enlisted in the U.S. Army. He was assigned to Avon Park Air Force Range in South-Central Florida. While in Florida, Catal filed for divorce from Rose Keating in March 1943. However, he neglected to indicate that he was domiciled in Florida as part of the divorce proceedings.

In July 1945, Catal returned to Wilkes-Barre on leave from the army. He and Anna applied for a marriage license on 25 July 1945. On that license, Catal stated that he had been previously married, and that a final decree for divorce had been granted in the State of Florida in August 1943. Catal and Anna were married on 26 July 1945 by Justice of the Peace W. Howell Evans in Wyoming, Pennsylvania.[68]

Since Catal had not established residence in Florida prior to his filing for divorce there, the State of Pennsylvania would not recognize the validity of the divorce. Though Rose did not respond to Catal's initial application for divorce, she nevertheless filed a complaint for bigamy against Catal once he remarried.

On 23 October 1945, Catal was indicted on the charge of bigamy. On 27 March 1946, "Judge W.A. Valentine found Catal guilty of bigamy because the divorce from his first wife was not valid."[69] In view of the court, the divorce was not valid because Catal never intended for Florida to be his permanent residence. Nor did he pay income taxes of vote in the State of Florida.

The whole course of events must have seemed absurd to Catal, who clearly wanted to move on with his life. There was much suffering due to one person's scorn.

His divorce from Rose Keating became final in the State of Pennsylvania, when on 27 November 1946 Docket number 893 in Luzerne County declared it so. He and Anna were re-married on 9 January 1947.[70]

Anna worked at the Presto Restaurant in Wilkes-Barre for the next 25 years. For his part, Catal continued his work as a master mechanic, finishing his career with the U.S. Postal Service in Wilkes-Barre. Together, they would have two sons, John, and Joseph (1951 – 2012). The Ormando family would often hold family reunions at Catal and Anna's summer residence in North Lake, Pennsylvania.

Catal passed away on 22 December 1981.[71] Anna outlived her husband by almost 20 years and died 2 May 2001.[72] They are buried together in St. Mary's Byzantine Catholic Cemetery in Dallas Township, Pennsylvania.

Lucille Leonardi

34 - Lucille Leonardi

Lucille Alice Leonardi was born 17 July 1924 to Gaetano and Mary Ormando Leonardi. She was the first of four daughters born to Gaetano and Mary between 1924 and 1936. Lucille and her family lived at 5 West Oak Street before moving to Main Street in the early 1940s. By 1943, the family resided at 225 South Main Street, where the family home would remain until 1984.

Lucille was part of the American-Italian generation of the Ormando family – those who were born in America, and became assimilated into American culture. Lucille bore the expectations of being the oldest sibling. She was expected to be a proper Italian girl and help her mother with her siblings.

There is a family story that when her youngest sibling, Virginia, was born, in January 1936, that Lucille went out on the front porch and cried. She was not crying because she now had another sister though.

The year 1936 was in the midst of the Great Depression. Her father did not have regular work, and Lucille was worried where the family would find the money to keep them fed. These are the worries that a twelve-year old child should never have to bear.

By the time she graduated from Pittston High School on 19 June 1942, the United States was embroiled in World War II. She found employment, through the National Recovery Act (NRA), as a Social Worker with the American Red Cross in Pittston, Pennsylvania. It was while she was working at the Red Cross that she would meet the man that she would marry.

Edward Anthony "Pier" Maziarz was born to Thomas and Mary Gawry Maziarz on 14 November 1909 in Duryea, Pennsylvania. Thomas and Mary emigrated from Poland in April 1905 via Hamburg, Germany. Edward was the third of five children, including William, Rose, Matthew, and Thomas. Following his graduation from high school in 1927, Edward worked as a coalminer for the Glen Alden Coal Company during the Depression.

35 - Edward "Pier" Maziarz

In June 1942, Edward enlisted in the U.S. Army and served as a Technical Sergeant in the 39th Infantry Division. On 15 November 1944, near Strasburg in France, he was wounded badly during battle. His recovery required eight months in military hospitals. For his wounds, Edward received the Purple Heart.

After the war, Edward purchased a building at 626 Main Street in Duryea, Pennsylvania, and setup an insurance business. There, he sold fire, casualty, and auto insurance. The business was a great success.

Edward entered into politics by becoming a Justice of the Peace in 1947. In 1948, he ran for the State Legislature in the sixth district that included Duryea, Pennsylvania. He ran as a Democrat in an overwhelmingly Republican district. Edward's charm and political acumen swayed the voters, and he was elected.

In 1950, Edward became the chair for the Democratic Party in the Sixth Legislative District. The Wilkes-Barre Sunday Independent noted, "Maziarz has an enviable war record. He entered service in 1942 in the army and served overseas for one year. He was injured in the Battle of the Bulge. [Edward] is an agreeable person all around."[73]

Lucille Leonardi and Edward Maziarz were married at Saint Rocco's Church in Pittston, Pennsylvania on 21 July 1952. Lucille's Aunt Susan Ormando was her maid of honor, while Edward's brother, Matthew, was his best man.

After his time as chair of the Democratic Party in the Sixth Legislative District, Edward served in many political positions in Luzerne County, including school board and tax appraiser. Lucille joined Edward in running their insurance business during this time, and Lucille learned politics from Edward. They were partners in everything that they did.

By 1960, Edward became a delegate to the Democratic National Convention, being held that year in Los Angeles, California. When John F. Kennedy became President of the United States in January 1961, Lucille and Edward were invited to Kennedy's inaugural ball. Lucille recalled how thrilling it was to be part of the inauguration festivities. It was also rewarding to her and Edward that his efforts in politics were being recognized at a national level.

Edward was once again a delegate to the Democratic Convention in 1964, and he continued to work in politics. Lucille and Edward also became part owners of the ZOM Construction Company.[74] The company built homes in the Duryea area. One of their projects became the Hillcrest Heights neighborhood of Duryea, Pennsylvania.

Tragedy struck the couple in early 1968. On 28 February 1968, Edward went to a meeting at the Polish Falcons Club where he was a member. Sometime that evening he suffered a massive cerebral hemorrhage. He died at 1:40 am on 1 March 1968. In the months prior to his death, Edward was elected as a delegate to the Democratic Convention in Chicago, Illinois that year.

Because he and Lucille were partners in everything, the Democratic Party extended that invitation to Lucille. I still revel in my Aunt Lucille's stories of her time at that convention, which was a seminal moment in our country's history.

The 1968 Democratic Convention in Chicago was an unfortunate reflection of life in America. Thousands of anti-war demonstrators had come to Chicago to disrupt the convention. They were protesting America's involvement in the Vietnam War and Hubert Humphrey's pro-war stance. The protests turned violent when law enforcement confronted the crowd. Some of that violence swept onto the floor of the Democratic Convention. Lucille managed to avoid becoming entangled in the melee, but she never forgot the scene at that convention.

Lucille was elected as a delegate to the Democratic Convention in 1972, 1976, and 1980. She was appointed to the Democratic National Credentials Committee in 1984 and again in 1988. She was elected as a delegate to the convention in 1992, and finally in 1996.

Lucille was also recognized as a stalwart of the Democratic Party in the State of Pennsylvania. She served as Councilwoman in Duryea, Pennsylvania from 1968 through 1986. Lucille also served as the Pittston Area School Director during her career.

Lucille graduated from the Wharton School of Business, and continued her insurance and construction businesses. She was licensed in both Real Estate and Insurance, through the Penn State University School of Insurance and Real Estate.

During my many discussions with her, I was always curious as to why she never re-married. She was always smart, attractive, and possessed a sharp wit.

The answer came to me during an interview I did with her for this book. Whenever the subject of the interview turned to Edward Maziarz, which was often, I got a sense of immense mutual respect and admiration that they had for each other. He is still with her today in everything that she does. I believe that she never wanted to disappoint her "Pier." She never did.

8 – Remains

The men who once mined the anthracite coal in the Wyoming Valley have passed on. The large collieries have passed into history as well. The scars on the land atop the mines and their surrounding areas, though, continue to haunt the Wyoming Valley to this day.

MINE SUBSIDENCE can cause the land to slide, buckle, or cave-in. The anthracite coal companies wanted to extract the product as quickly and cheaply as possible. This often meant improperly supporting the mine interiors, digging tunnels one on top of the other, shafts that were improperly filled, and mining too closely to the surface.

The problem of mine subsidence had been known since the late 1800's. "In many places near Wilkes-Barre, in Pittston, Hyde Park and in Kingston large areas of land undermined have subsided by the caving in of mines…The large brick schoolhouse near Pittston, at the corner of the road to Yatesville, was abandoned because the walls cracked so as to be dangerous to pupils, the supports of the mines below having failed."[75]

The home that Mary Leonardi Ormando lived in at 225 South Main Street in Pittston, Pennsylvania suffered severe damage due to mine subsidence in the Spring of 1981. As fate would have it, her home sat directly atop of an old mine shaft from the Pennsylvania Coal Company that had long been abandoned.

In early March, a small hole formed under the back porch of the home. It was the first sign the a mine subsidence had begun. By 14 April 1981, the hole had become 25 feet wide and about 60 feet deep. Portions of the cellar were swallowed up by the subsidence, as was the rear foundation of the house[76].

Mary was forced to evacuate her house on orders from the Pennsylvania Office of Surface Mining. For a time, there was concern that the house might tip over onto the house next door at 221 South Main Street. Fortunately that potential disaster was averted.

Steel beams, ordinarily used to erect buildings were brought in to stabilize the foundation. It was then the Office of Surface Mining was able to backfill the hole and allow the home to be reoccupied.

Mine subsidence continues to plague Northeastern Pennsylvania, in part because of a plethora of abandoned mines. Not all of these mines are well marked or well mapped. Insurance is available to protect homeowners from the damage due to subsidence. However, this is small comfort when a mine subsidence consumes your yard, or entire house.

UNDERGROUND COALMINE FIRES are another hazard that remains from the King Coal era. The town of Centralia, Pennsylvania became victim to an underground coalmine fire in 1962. Fire from the legal burning of a trash dump unintentionally extended to an underground coal seam. The fire still burns today.

36 - Warning sign outside of the abandoned town of Centralia, Pennsylvania (public domain)

While the people of the town of Centralia were exposed to the dangers of the mine fire for twenty years, no federal or state agency seemed interested in their plight. That is, no one wanted to pay for the cost of controlling the fire or evacuating the townspeople. It was always someone else's problem.

It seemed that no government entity cared that the miners and their families were being exposed to carbon dioxide, carbon monoxide, and hydrogen sulfide. For twenty-two years, the people of this small hamlet were almost entirely ignored.

The town of Centralia was finally abandoned in 1984. The United States Congress appropriated over $42 million to relocate the 1,000 plus residents of the town. In 1992, the Commonwealth of Pennsylvania seized the buildings in

Centralia, and promptly condemned them all. The zip code for the town was removed by the U.S. Postal Service in 2002.

For all intent, Centralia no longer exists. Today, warning signs are posted warning anyone who would stray to closely to the affected area. The ghosts of the anthracite coal companies and their miners still linger in many places northeastern Pennsylvania.

37 - An empty street in the ghost town of Centralia.

9 – Epilogue

THE LAST of the second generation of the Ormando family passed away in 1972. Only a handful remains from the third generation – those that became integrated into the American way of life, yet retained some of the culture and customs of the old world. Were their lives better than those of the previous generation were?

Fourteen of the sixteen males from the third generation of the Ormando family finished high school, and one of those went on to college. Therefore, they were better educated than their parents were. Their average life span of 79 years was two years longer than their father's lives. Some of the men from this generation worked sporadically in the mines, but none born after 1908 worked their entire career in the coalmines.

For the women, only three of twelve from this thrid generation finished high school and none went onto college. Women were still expected to be homemakers first. Everything else was secondary in importance.

Yet, some, like Grace Amico, made her living for many years in the garment industry. She was also one of two women of her generation that never married.[77] Though they lived an average of six years longer than their mothers did, it would be a stretch to say that their quality of life was significantly better.

The fourth generation of the Ormando family – Gaetano Ormando's great-grandchildren – is where one begins to see life getting discernibly better. Most members of this generation held white-collar jobs, and many of the women had successful careers as well.

It is with this generation that the vision held by the first generation of the Ormando family in America, finally became a reality. Life was better for the fourth generation of the family.

They owned their own homes, attended college, and raised families. Family surnames now include many non-Italian names such as Novak, Bonner, Barr, Reese, Maziarz, Drexinger, Dudzik, and O'Connor.

Upon visiting Sicily, my mother and her three sisters discovered that life there has undergone a similar transition. Ormando relatives in Sicily have become doctors, teachers, orchestra conductors, and owners of small businesses.

The Ormando family came to the Wyoming Valley in Luzerne County, Pennsylvania with a desire for a better life. For their descendants, that dream of a better life has become a reality.

Afterword

IT WAS the end of June 1962, and my mother Virginia Leonardi Novak had taken my brother and me to visit our grandparents, Gaetano and Mary Ormando Leonardi in Pittston. We were there to help celebrate my grandmother's birthday on July 3, and go to Fanti's Park for an Ormando family get together that day as well. My father was serving his two-week commitment in the U.S. Army Reserve at the time. Also in town for a visit that weekend were my Aunt Helen, Uncle Clifford, and their daughter Helen.

38 - The author with his cousin Helen O'Connor, 30 June 1962

July 1, 1962 started out much like most other Sundays at 225 South Main Street in Pittston, Pennsylvania. After returning from mass at Saint Rocco's, relatives would stop by to say hello, and everyone was making plans for the big family get together later that afternoon at Fanti's Park. Before going to the family reunion; however, the children needed to take a nap.

The room I was to take a nap in was the second bedroom on the second floor and my bed was next to the window. That window was open because, like most July days in Pittston, it was hot. Moreover, like most kids who are supposed to be taking a nap, I was not napping. Instead, I was playing with my stuffed dog. In the course of my playing, the dog got too near the window and went out. I must have reached for the stuffed animal to save it from falling because I probably did not want to get into trouble. However, I reached too far.

Now, that second floor window was actually three stories up because of the way the ground slopped away from the house as it went toward the back of the house. In an instant, I went hurtling to the ground. My grandmother, who was making pasta to take to the reunion, saw me falling toward the ground and started screaming hysterically. It was not until my mother and my Aunt Helen looked outside and saw what had happened to me that the rest of the family was alerted.

I was initially taken to Pittston Hospital because of the severity of my injuries. When I was stabilized one week later, I was transferred to Geisinger Hospital in Danville, Pennsylvania. These injuries included a compound skull fracture and a crushed right tear duct. The doctors told my parents that they would do all they could, but could not assure them that I would survive, or if I survived I would probably suffered permanent brain damage.

As it turned out, it was the compound fracture (a puncture wound) of my skull that saved my life. The compound fracture relieved the pressure on my brain that would have otherwise killed me, or at the very least rendered me incapable of doing anything for myself for as long as I might have lived. Today, I am known throughout the Ormando family as "the boy who fell out the window."

Pedigree Charts

The following pedigree charts correspond to the family members whose stories are highlighted in the biographical vignettes, as well as that of the author.

Pedigree Chart for Nellie Amico

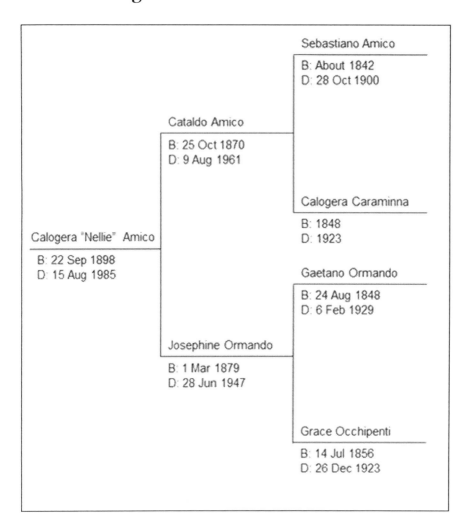

Calogera "Nellie" Amico
B: 22 Sep 1898
D: 15 Aug 1985

Cataldo Amico
B: 25 Oct 1870
D: 9 Aug 1961

Josephine Ormando
B: 1 Mar 1879
D: 28 Jun 1947

Sebastiano Amico
B: About 1842
D: 28 Oct 1900

Calogera Caraminna
B: 1848
D: 1923

Gaetano Ormando
B: 24 Aug 1848
D: 6 Feb 1929

Grace Occhipenti
B: 14 Jul 1856
D: 26 Dec 1923

Pedigree Chart for Stephen Bellanca

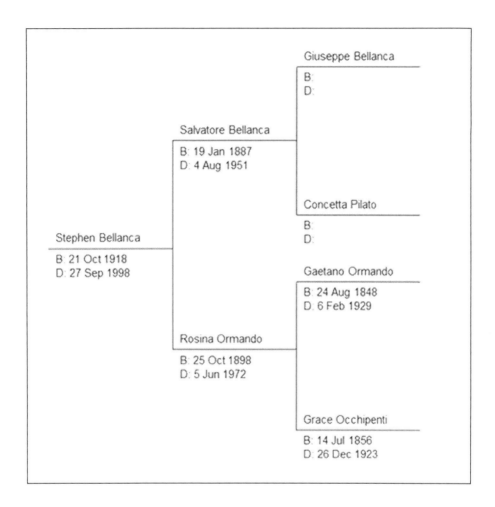

Pedigree Chart for Ross Prizzi

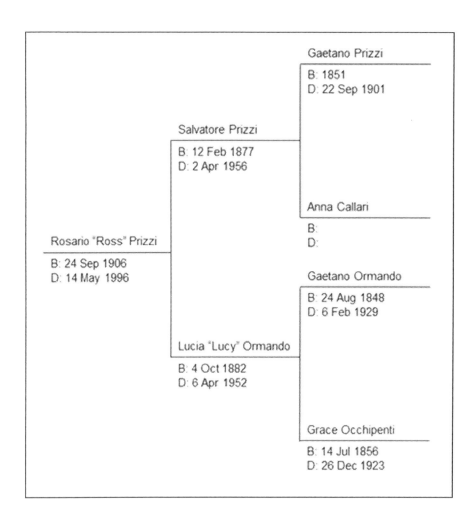

Pedigree Chart for Mary DiLorenzo

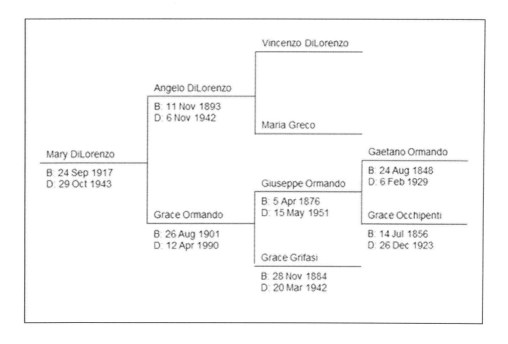

Pedigree Chart for Catal Ormando

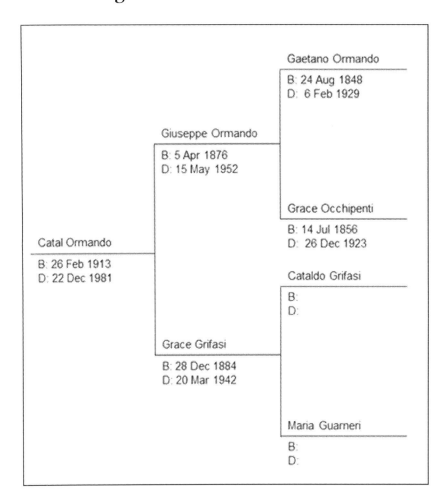

Pedigree Chart for Lucille Leonardi

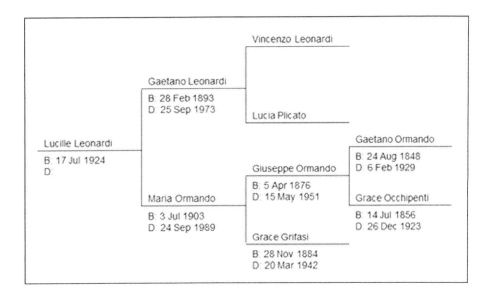

Pedigree Chart for Martin Novak (author)

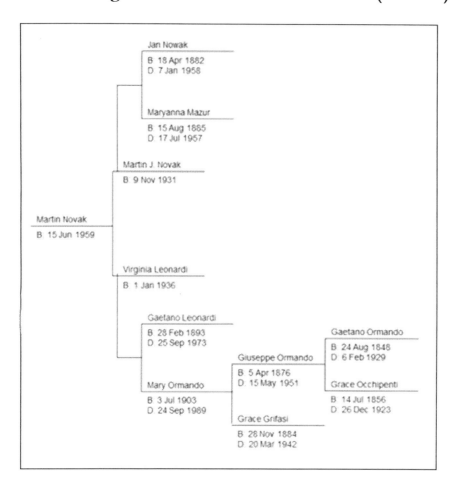

Descendants of Gaetano Ormando

First Generation

1. **Gaetano Ormando** was born on 24 Aug 1848 in San Cataldo, Caltanissetta, Sicily, Italy. He died on 6 Feb 1929 in West Wyoming, Luzerne, Pennsylvania.

Gaetano Ormando and Grace Occhipenti were married on 3 Aug 1873 in San Cataldo, Caltanissetta, Sicily, Italy. **Grace Occhipenti**, daughter of Giovanni Occhipenti and Lucia Amico, was born on 14 Jul 1856 in San Cataldo, Caltanissetta, Sicily, Italy. She died on 26 Dec 1923 in Pittston, Luzerne, Pennsylvania.

Gaetano Ormando and Grace Occhipenti had the following children:

2	i.	**Giuseppe "Joseph" Ormando**, born 5 Apr 1876, San Cataldo, Caltanissetta, Sicily, Italy; died 15 May 1951, Pittston, Luzerne, Pennsylvania.
3	ii.	**Josephine Ormando**, born 7 Apr 1879, San Cataldo, Caltanissetta, Sicily, Italy; died 28 Jun 1947, Pittston, Luzerne, Pennsylvania.
4	iii.	**Lucia "Lucy" Ormando**, born 15 Oct 1882, San Cataldo, Caltanissetta, Sicily, Italy; died 6 Apr 1952, Swoyersville, Luzerne, Pennsylvania.
	iv.	**Maria Ormando** was born on 28 Jun 1885 in San Cataldo, Caltanissetta, Sicily, Italy. She died stillborn on 28 Jun 1885 at the age of 0 in San Cataldo, Caltanissetta, Sicily, Italy.
5	v.	**Giovanni "John" Ormando**, born 30 Jan 1888, San Cataldo, Caltanissetta, Sicily, Italy; died 27 Mar 1964, Pittston, Luzerne, Pennsylvania.
	vi.	**Salvatore Ormando** was born on 4 Aug 1890 in San Cataldo, Caltanissetta, Sicily, Italy. He died on 11 Sep 1892 at the age of 2 in San Cataldo, Caltanissetta, Sicily, Italy.
	vii.	**Salvatore Ormando** was born on 28 Feb 1893 in San Cataldo, Caltanissetta, Sicily, Italy. He died on 3 Nov 1893 at the age of 0 in San Cataldo, Caltanissetta, Sicily, Italy.
6	viii.	**Maria "Mary" Ormando**, born 9 Jun 1895, San Cataldo, Caltanissetta, Sicily, Italy; died 18 Feb 1980, Wyoming, Luzerne, Pennsylvania.
7	ix.	**Rosina "Rose" Ormando**, born 26 Oct 1898, San Cataldo, Caltanissetta, Sicily, Italy; she died 5 Jun 1973, Pittston, Luzerne, Pennsylvania.

Second Generation

2. **Giuseppe "Joseph" Ormando** (Gaetano-1) was born on 5 Apr 1876 in San Cataldo, Caltanissetta, Sicily, Italy. He died on 15 May 1951 at the age of 75 in Pittston, Luzerne, Pennsylvania.

Giuseppe "Joseph" Ormando and Grace Ann Grifasi were married on 15 Sep 1900 in San Cataldo, Caltanissetta, Sicily, Italy. **Grace Ann Grifasi**, daughter of Cataldo Grifasi and Maria Guarneri, was born on 28 Nov 1884 in San Cataldo, Caltanissetta, Sicily, She died on 20 Mar 1942 in Pittston, Luzerne, Pennsylvania.

Giuseppe Ormando and Grace Ann Grifasi had the following children:

8	i.	**Grazia "Grace" Ormando**, born 26 Aug 1901, San Cataldo, Caltanissetta, Sicily, Italy; died 12 Apr 1990, Pittston, Luzerne, Pennsylvania.
9	ii.	**Mary Ormando**, born 3 Jul 1903, San Cataldo, Caltanissetta, Sicily, Italy; died 24 Sep 1989, Wilkes-Barre, Luzerne, Pennsylvania.
	iii.	**Providenzia Ormando** was born on 27 Oct 1906 in San Cataldo, Caltanissetta, Sicily, Italy. She died on 10 May 1907 at the age of 0 in San Cataldo, Caltanissetta, Sicily, Italy.
10	iv.	**Gaetano "Tony" Ormando**, born 26 Apr 1908, San Cataldo, Caltanissetta, Sicily, Italy; died 28 Apr 1982, North Bergen, Hudson, New Jersey.
	v.	**Assunta Ormando** was born after 1909 in San Cataldo, Caltanissetta, Sicily, Italy. She died before 1912 at the age of 3 in San Cataldo, Caltanissetta, Sicily, Italy.
11	vi.	**Catal James "Ky" Ormando**, born 26 Feb 1913, San Cataldo, Caltanissetta, Sicily, Italy; died 22 Dec 1981, Wilkes-Barre, Luzerne, Pennsylvania.
12	vii.	**Carmela Rita Ormando**, born 5 Oct 1915, Pittston, Luzerne, Pennsylvania; died 2 Apr 1995, Easton, Northampton, Pennsylvania.
13	viii.	**Susan "Sue" Ormando**, born 16 Feb 1918, Pittston, Luzerne, Pennsylvania; died 29 Apr 1991, Pittston, Luzerne, Pennsylvania.
14	ix.	**Josephine Ormando**, born 25 Dec 1919, Pittston, Luzerne, Pennsylvania; died 24 Oct 1994, Pittston, Luzerne, Pennsylvania.
15	x.	**James Ormando**, born 30 Jan 1921, Pittston, Luzerne, Pennsylvania; died 20 May 2001, Pittston, Luzerne, Pennsylvania.
16	xi.	**John Joseph Ormando**, born 7 Nov 1923, Pittston, Luzerne, Pennsylvania; died 1 Jul 2005, Pittston, Luzerne, Pennsylvania.

3. **Josephine Ormando** (Gaetano-1) was born on 7 Apr 1879 in San Cataldo, Caltanissetta, Sicily, Italy. She died on 28 Jun 1947 in Pittston, Luzerne, Pennsylvania.

Josephine Ormando and Cataldo Amico were married on 13 Jun 1896 in San Cataldo, Caltanissetta, Sicily, Italy. **Cataldo Amico**, son of Sebastiano Amico and Calogera Caraminna, was born on 25 Oct 1870 in San Cataldo, Caltanissetta, Sicily, Italy. He died on 9 Aug 1961 at the age of 90 in Pittston, Luzerne, Pennsylvania.

Cataldo Amico and Josephine Ormando had the following children:

17	i.	**Calogera "Nellie" Amico**, born 22 Sep 1898, San Cataldo, Caltanissetta, Sicily, Italy; died 15 Aug 1985, in Pittston, Luzerne, Pennsylvania.
	ii.	**Sebastiano Amico** was born on 18 Jul 1901 in San Cataldo, Caltanissetta, Sicily, Italy. He died on 22 Sep 1901 at the age of 0 in San Cataldo, Caltanissetta, Sicily, Italy.
18	iii.	**Sebastiano N. "Sam" Amico**, born 3 Feb 1906, Pittston, Luzerne, Pennsylvania; died 5 Sep 1977, in Pittston, Luzerne, Pennsylvania.
	iv.	**Grace Amico** was born on 3 Jan 1909 in Pittston, Luzerne, Pennsylvania. She died on 4 Dec 2001 in Wyoming, Luzerne, Pennsylvania.
19	v.	**Gaetano "Tony" Amico**, born 3 Jan 1911, Pittston, Luzerne, Pennsylvania; died 24 Jan 1982, Clifton Springs, Ontario, New York of America.
20	vi.	**Joseph Amico**, born 29 Jul 1914, Pittston, Luzerne, Pennsylvania; died 4 Feb 2007, Pittston, Luzerne, Pennsylvania.
21	vii.	**Matthew Amadeo Amico**, born 23 Apr 1919, Pittston, Luzerne, Pennsylvania; died 30 Jun 2009, Pittston, Luzerne, Pennsylvania.
22	viii.	**Louis T. Amico**, born 23 Oct 1921, Pittston, Luzerne, Pennsylvania; died 17 Jun 1990, Swoyersville, Luzerne, Pennsylvania.

4. **Lucia "Lucy" Ormando** (Gaetano-1) was born on 15 Oct 1882 in San Cataldo, Caltanissetta, Sicily, Italy. She died on 6 Apr 1952 at the age of 69 in Swoyersville, Luzerne, Pennsylvania.

Lucia "Lucy" Ormando and Salvatore "Sam" Prizzi were married on 16 Dec 1899 in San Cataldo, Caltanissetta, Sicily, Italy. **Salvatore "Sam" Prizzi**, son of Gaetano Prizzi and Anna Callari, was born on 12 Feb 1877 in San Cataldo, Caltanissetta, Sicily, Italy. He died on 2 Apr 1956 in Jenkins, Luzerne, Pennsylvania.

Salvatore Prizzi and Lucia Ormando had the following children:

23	i.	**Anthony Prizzi**, born 12 Sep 1901, San Cataldo, Caltanissetta, Sicily, Italy; died Jan 1972, Wyoming, Luzerne, Pennsylvania.
24	ii.	**Anna Prizzi**, born 15 Aug 1904, Pittston, Luzerne, Pennsylvania; died 15 Aug 1976, Easton, Northampton, Pennsylvania.
25	iii.	**Rosario Calogero "Ross" Prizzi**, born 28 Sep 1906, San Cataldo, Caltanissetta, Sicily, Italy; died 14 May 1996, Old Forge, Lackawanna, Pennsylvania.

5. **Giovanni "John" Ormando** (Gaetano-1) was born on 30 Jan 1888 in San Cataldo, Caltanissetta, Sicily, Italy. He died on 27 Mar 1964 at the age of 76 in Pittston, Luzerne, Pennsylvania.

Giovanni "John" Ormando and Calogera Grifasi were married on 18 May 1907 in San Cataldo, Caltanissetta, Sicily, Italy. **Calogera Grifasi**, daughter of Cataldo Grifasi and Maria Guarneri, was born on 28 Mar 1889 in San Cataldo, Caltanissetta, Sicily, Italy. She died in 1910 in San Cataldo, Caltanissetta, Sicily, Italy.

Giovanni "John" Ormando and Rosaria "Sara" Pilato were married on 10 Dec 1910 in San Cataldo, Caltanissetta, Sicily, Italy. **Rosaria "Sara" Pilato**, daughter of Salvatore Pilato and Teresa Mastrosimone, was born on 16 Feb 1892 in San Cataldo, Caltanissetta, Sicily, Italy. She died in Oct 1970 in Pittston, Luzerne, Pennsylvania.

Giovanni Ormando and Rosaria "Sara" Pilato had the following child:

    26   i. **Anthony Ormando**, born 26 Feb 1915, Pittston, Luzerne, Pennsylvania; died 1994, Toms River, Ocean, New Jersey.

6. **Maria "Mary" Ormando** (Gaetano-1) was born on 9 Jun 1895 in San Cataldo, Caltanissetta, Sicily, Italy. Mary died on 18 Feb 1980 in Wyoming, Luzerne, Pennsylvania.

Maria "Mary" Ormando and Concetto "Frank" Agati were married on 6 Feb 1910 in Pittston, Luzerne, Pennsylvania. **Concetto "Frank" Agati**, son of Antonino Agati and Lucia DiSilvestro, was born on 11 Jun 1888 in San Cataldo, Caltanissetta, Sicily, Italy. He died on 16 Feb 1928 in Wilkes-Barre, Luzerne, Pennsylvania.

Concetto "Frank" Agati and Maria Ormando had the following children:

	i.	**Antonino Agati** was born on 25 Nov 1911 in Pittston, Luzerne, Pennsylvania. He died on 27 Mar 1914 at the age of 2 in Pittston, Luzerne, Pennsylvania.
	ii.	**Lucy C. Agati** was born on 7 Dec 1913 in Pittston, Luzerne, Pennsylvania. She died on 20 Dec 1995 at the age of 82 in Kingston, Luzerne, Pennsylvania.
27	iii.	**Anthony "Nino" Agati**, born 8 Nov 1915, Pittston, Luzerne, Pennsylvania; died 18 May 1990, Philadelphia, Pennsylvania.
28	iv.	**Grace Agati**, born 21 Nov 1917, Pittston, Luzerne, Pennsylvania; died 25 Oct 2008, Pittston, Luzerne, Pennsylvania.
29	v.	**Angelina Agati**, born 19 Aug 1919, Pittston, Luzerne, Pennsylvania; died 29 May 1984, Wyoming, Luzerne, Pennsylvania.
30	vi.	**Guy Angelo Agati**, born 23 May 1921, Pittston, Luzerne, Pennsylvania; died 5 Apr 1985, Kingston, Luzerne, Pennsylvania.
31	vii.	**Sarah Agati**
32	viii.	**Josephine Agati**

7. **Rosina "Rose" Ormando** (Gaetano-1) was born on 26 Oct 1898 in San Cataldo, Caltanissetta, Sicily, Italy. Rose died on 5 Jun 1973 in Pittston, Luzerne, Pennsylvania.

Rosina "Rose" Ormando and Salvatore "Sam" Bellanca were married in Jun 1913 in San Cataldo, Caltanissetta, Sicily, Italy. **Salvatore "Sam" Bellanca**, son of Giuseppe Bellanca and Concetta Pilato, was born on 19 Jan 1887 in San Cataldo, Caltanissetta, Sicily, Italy. He died on 4 Aug 1951 in Jenkins, Luzerne, Pennsylvania.

Salvatore Bellanca and Rosina Ormando had the following children:

33	i.	**Joseph L. Bellanca**, born 10 Jul 1914, Pittston, Luzerne, Pennsylvania; died 20 Oct 1994, Wilkes-Barre, Luzerne, Pennsylvania.
34	ii.	**Anthony Angelo Bellanca**, born 2 Dec 1916, Pittston, Luzerne, Pennsylvania; died 16 Jul 1994, Wyoming, Luzerne, Pennsylvania.
35	iii.	**Stephen L. Bellanca**, born 21 Oct 1918, Pittston, Luzerne, Pennsylvania; died 27 Sep 1998, Wilkes-Barre, Luzerne, Pennsylvania.
36	iv.	**Concetta Marie "Connie" Bellanca**
37	v.	**Samuel Bellanca Jr.**

Third Generation

8. **Grazia "Grace" Ormando** (Giuseppe-2, Gaetano-1) was born on 26 Aug 1901 in San Cataldo, Caltanissetta, Sicily, Italy. She died on 12 Apr 1990 in Pittston, Luzerne, Pennsylvania.

Grazia "Grace" Ormando and Angelo DiLorenzo were married on 10 Sep 1916 in Pittston, Luzerne, Pennsylvania. **Angelo DiLorenzo**, son of Vincenzo Di Lorenzo and Maria Greco, was born on 11 Nov 1893 in Serradifalco, Caltanissetta, Sicily, Italy. He died on 6 Nov 1942 in Pittston, Luzerne, Pennsylvania.

Angelo DiLorenzo and Grazia Ormando had the following children:

38	i.	**Mary DiLorenzo**, born 24 Sep 1917, Pittston, Luzerne, Pennsylvania; died 29 Oct 1943, Wilkes-Barre, Luzerne, Pennsylvania.
	ii.	**Grace DiLorenzo** was born on 28 Feb 1919 in Pittston, Luzerne, Pennsylvania. She died on 27 Jan 1942 in Pittston, Luzerne, Pennsylvania.
39	iii.	**Rose Mary DiLorenzo**
40	iv.	**Frances DiLorenzo**, born 25 Jun 1922, Pittston, Luzerne, Pennsylvania; died 12 Oct 2008, Pittston, Luzerne, Pennsylvania.
41	v.	**James Peter "Jimmy" DiLorenzo**, born 9 Oct 1926, Pittston, Luzerne, Pennsylvania; died 3 Oct 2009, Exeter, Luzerne, Pennsylvania.
42	vi.	**Joseph James "Joe" DiLorenzo**, born 5 Oct 1930, Pittston, Luzerne, Pennsylvania; died 24 Nov 2010, Saint Petersburg, Pinellas, Florida.

9. **Mary Ormando** (Giuseppe-2, Gaetano-1) was born on 3 Jul 1903 in San Cataldo, Caltanissetta, Sicily, Italy. Mary died on 24 Sep 1989 at the age of 86 in Wilkes-Barre, Luzerne, Pennsylvania.

Mary Ormando and Gaetano Leonardi were married on 15 Jul 1923 in Pittston, Luzerne, Pennsylvania. **Gaetano Leonardi**, son of Vincenzo Leonardi and Lucia Pilicato, was born on 28 Feb 1893 in San Cataldo, Caltanissetta, Sicily, Italy. He died on 25 Sep 1973 at the age of 80 in Pittston, Luzerne, Pennsylvania.

Gaetano Leonardi and Mary Ormando had the following children:

43	i.	**Lucille Alice Leonardi**
44	ii.	**Grace Leonardi**
45	iii.	**Helen Leonardi**
46	iv.	**Virginia Elaine Leonardi**

10. **Gaetano "Tony" Ormando** (Giuseppe-2, Gaetano-1) was born on 26 Apr 1908 in San Cataldo, Caltanissetta, Sicily, Italy. He died on 28 Apr 1982 at the age of 74 in North Bergen, Hudson, New Jersey.

Gaetano "Tony" Ormando and Mollie DePascale were married on 10 Sep 1938 in Pittston, Luzerne, Pennsylvania. **Mollie DePascale**, daughter of Silvio DePascale and Louise Bianco, was born on 2 Sep 1914 in Jenkins, Luzerne, Pennsylvania. She died on 12 May 1996 at the age of 81 in Brick Township, Ocean, New Jersey.

Gaetano Ormando and Mollie DePascale had the following children:

      47   i. **Grace Ormando**
      48   ii. **Joseph William Ormando**
      49   iii. **James John Ormando**
           iv. **Sylvia Marie Ormando**

11. **Catal James "Ky" Ormando** (Giuseppe-2, Gaetano-1) was born on 26 Feb 1913 in San Cataldo, Caltanissetta, Sicily, Italy. He died on 22 Dec 1981 at the age of 68 in Wilkes-Barre, Luzerne, Pennsylvania.

Catal James "Ky" Ormando and Rose Keating were married on 12 Apr 1934 in Pittston, Luzerne, Pennsylvania. They were divorced on 27 Nov 1946 in Wilkes-Barre, Luzerne, Pennsylvania. **Rose Keating**, daughter of John J. Keating and Mary Devers, was born on 2 Mar 1907 in Pittston, Luzerne, Pennsylvania. She died on 7 Mar 1980 at the age of 73 in Pittston, Luzerne, Pennsylvania.

Catal James Ormando and Rose Keating had the following children:

      50   i. **Rosalie Ormando**
           ii. **Margaret M. Ormando**

Catal James "Ky" Ormando and Anna Kerchanin were married on 9 Jan 1947 in Wyoming, Luzerne, Pennsylvania. **Anna Kerchanin**, daughter of John Kerchanin and Mary Onesko, was born on 20 Dec 1916 in Wilkes-Barre, Luzerne, Pennsylvania. Anna died on 2 May 2001 at the age of 84 in Wilkes-Barre, Luzerne, Pennsylvania.

Catal James Ormando and Anna Kerchanin had the following children:

      51   i. **John J. "Jack" Ormando**
      52   ii. **Joseph John Ormando**, born 15 Jan 1951, Pittston, Luzerne, Pennsylvania; died 31 Jan 2012, Wilkes-Barre, Luzerne, Pennsylvania.

12. **Carmela Rita Ormando** (Giuseppe-2, Gaetano-1) was born on 5 Oct 1915 in Pittston, Luzerne, Pennsylvania. She died on 2 Apr 1995 at the age of 79 in Easton, Northampton, Pennsylvania.

Carmela Rita Ormando and Franklin Charles "Frank" Barr were married in 1937 in Pennsylvania. They were divorced about 1951 in Easton, Northampton, Pennsylvania. **Franklin Charles Barr**, son of Daniel Barr and Elizabeth Mosier, was born on 5 Dec 1907 in East Stroudsburg, Monroe, Pennsylvania. He died on 10 Nov 1990 at the age of 82 in East Stroudsburg, Monroe, Pennsylvania.

Franklin Charles Barr and Carmela Rita Ormando had the following children:

53	i.	**Daniel Barr**, born 4 May 1938, East Stroudsburg, Monroe, Pennsylvania; died 31 Jul 2002, East Stroudsburg, Monroe, Pennsylvania.
54	ii.	**Catal Barr**
55	iii.	**Elizabeth Barr**, born 26 May 1941, Easton, Northampton, Pennsylvania; died 30 Mar 2013, Washington Township, Northampton, Pennsylvania.
56	iv.	**Rosemary Barr**
57	v.	**Jacqueline Barr**
58	vi.	**Bernadette "Kitty" Barr**

Carmela Rita Ormando and Joseph Davanzo were married about 1955. **Joseph Davanzo**, son of Donato Davanzo and Carmela Figlioli, was born on 18 Feb 1908. died in Aug 1983 at the age of 75 in Portland, Northampton, Pennsylvania of America.

13. **Susan "Sue" Ormando** (Giuseppe-2, Gaetano-1) was born on 16 Feb 1918 in Pittston, Luzerne, Pennsylvania. She died on 29 Apr 1991 at the age of 73 in Pittston, Luzerne, Pennsylvania.

Susan "Sue" Ormando and Max Howard McCuen were married in 1959. They were divorced in Oct 1966 in Los Angeles, Los Angeles, California. **Max Howard McCuen**, son of Leander J. McCuen and Louisa Townsend, was born on 31 Aug 1912 in Atlantic, Cass, Iowa. He died on 11 Jul 1979 at the age of 66 in Orange County, California, USA.

14. **Josephine Ormando** (Giuseppe-2, Gaetano-1) was born on 25 Dec 1919 in Pittston, Luzerne, Pennsylvania. She died on 24 Oct 1994 at the age of 74 in Pittston, Luzerne, Pennsylvania.

Josephine Ormando and John C. Adonizio were married on 6 Dec 1941 in Pittston, Luzerne, Pennsylvania. **John C. Adonizio**, son of Joseph Adonizio and Josephine Nardone, was born on 3 Oct 1909 in Pittston, Luzerne, Pennsylvania. He died on 23 Jan 1991 at the age of 81 in Swoyersville, Luzerne, Pennsylvania.

John C. Adonizio and Josephine Ormando had the following children:

	i.	**Joseph Adonizio**
59	ii.	**John W. Adonizio**
60	iii.	**Patrick J. Adonizio**

15. **James Ormando** (Giuseppe-2, Gaetano-1) was born on 30 Jan 1921 in Pittston, Luzerne, Pennsylvania. He died on 20 May 2001 at the age of 80 in Pittston, Luzerne, Pennsylvania.

James Ormando and Josephine Collura were married about 1953 in Pittston, Luzerne, Pennsylvania. **Josephine Collura**, daughter of Phillip Collura and Frances Algozina, was born in Plains, Luzerne, Pennsylvania.

James Ormando and Josephine Collura had the following child:

      i. **Susan Ormando**

16. **John Joseph Ormando** (Giuseppe-2, Gaetano-1) was born on 7 Nov 1923 in Pittston, Luzerne, Pennsylvania. He died on 1 Jul 2005 at the age of 81 in Pittston, Luzerne, Pennsylvania.

John Joseph Ormando and Theresa Butera were married on 12 Jul 1952 at St. Rocco's Italian Catholic Church in Pittston, Luzerne, Pennsylvania. **Theresa Butera**, daughter of Cataldo Butera and Carrie Angelo, was born in Pittston, Luzerne, Pennsylvania.

John Joseph Ormando and Theresa Butera had the following children:

61	i.	**John Ormando Jr.**
62	ii.	**Mary Teresa Ormando**

17. **Calogera "Nellie" Amico** (Josephine Ormando-2, Gaetano-1) was born on 22 Sep 1898 in San Cataldo, Caltanissetta, Sicily, Italy. She died on 15 Aug 1985 at the age of 86 in Pittston, Luzerne, Pennsylvania.

Calogera "Nellie" Amico and Cataldo Giannone were married on 21 Sep 1913 in Pittston, Luzerne, Pennsylvania. **Cataldo Giannone**, son of Salvatore Giannone and Rosaria Calabrice, was born on 23 Oct 1886 in San Cataldo, Caltanissetta, Sicily, Italy. Cataldo died on 15 Sep 1919 at the age of 32 in Pittston, Luzerne, Pennsylvania.

Cataldo Giannone and Calogera "Nellie" Amico had the following children:

63	i.	**Samuel John Giannone**, born 5 Dec 1915, Pittston, Luzerne, Pennsylvania; married Helen Emily Armusik, 4 Mar 1938, Pittston, Luzerne, Pennsylvania; died Sep 1967, Wyoming, Luzerne, Pennsylvania.
64	ii.	**Rosaria Sadie Giannone**, born 4 Mar 1918, Pittston, Luzerne, Pennsylvania; died 29 Mar 1994, Pittston, Luzerne, Pennsylvania.

Calogera "Nellie" Amico and Michele Aquilina were married on 24 Nov 1923 in Pittston, Luzerne, Pennsylvania. **Michele Aquilina**, son of Calogero Aquilina and Angela Bunaro, was born on 19 Mar 1888 in Serradifalco, Caltanissetta, Sicily, Italy. Michele died on 18 Jan 1940 at the age of 51 in Pittston, Luzerne, Pennsylvania.

Michele Aquilina and Calogera "Nellie" Amico had the following children:

	i.	**Cataldo "Ky" Aquilina** was born on 28 Jan 1925 in Pittston, Luzerne, Pennsylvania. He died on 26 Jul 1997 at the age of 72 in Plainview, Nassau, New York.
65	ii.	**Josephine Sara Aquilina**
66	iii.	**Anthony "Tony" Aquilina**
	iv.	**Joseph Aquilina**
	v.	**Vincent Aquilina**

18. **Sebastiano N. "Sam" Amico** (Josephine Ormando-2, Gaetano-1) was born on 3 Feb 1906 in Pittston, Luzerne, Pennsylvania. He died on 5 Sep 1977 at the age of 71 in Pittston, Luzerne, Pennsylvania.

Sebastiano N. "Sam" Amico and Inez Agnes Spiccioli were married on 7 Aug 1943 in Pittston, Luzerne, Pennsylvania. **Inez Agnes Spiccioli**, daughter of Joseph Spiccioli and Caroline Marinangeli, was born in Pittston, Luzerne, Pennsylvania.

Sebastiano N. Amico and Inez Agnes Spiccioli had the following children:

67	i.	**Stephen Amico**
68	ii.	**Josephine Amico**

19. **Gaetano "Tony" Amico** (Josephine Ormando-2, Gaetano-1) was born on 3 Jan 1911 in Pittston, Luzerne, Pennsylvania. He died on 24 Jan 1982 at the age of 71 in Clifton Springs, Ontario, New York of America.

Gaetano Amico had the following child:

69	i.	**Joann Amico**

Gaetano "Tony" Amico and Catherine Anne Bush were married about 1946.

Gaetano Amico and Catherine Anne Bush had the following children:

70	i.	**Dante Edward Amico**
	ii.	**Michael Amico**

Gaetano "Tony" Amico and Sybill Grey Walker were married on 12 Nov 1960 in Geneva, Seneca, New York. **Sybill Grey Walker** was born on 30 Nov 1923 in Beaufort, North Carolina. She died on 24 Sep 2000 at the age of 76 in Pamlico, North Carolina.

20. **Joseph Amico** (Josephine Ormando-2, Gaetano-1) was born on 29 Jul 1914 in Pittston, Luzerne, Pennsylvania. Joseph died on 4 Feb 2007 at the age of 92 in Pittston, Luzerne, Pennsylvania.

Joseph Amico and Josephine Polit were married on 11 Oct 1941 in Pittston, Luzerne, Pennsylvania. **Josephine Polit**, daughter of Salvatore "Sam" Ippolito and Maria Perelli, was born on 27 Nov 1916 in Pittston, Luzerne, Pennsylvania. She died on 10 Oct 2004 at the age of 87 in Pittston, Luzerne, Pennsylvania.

Joseph Amico and Josephine Polit had the following children:

    71   i. **Cataldo Amico**
    72   ii. **Josephine Amico**

21. **Matthew Amadeo Amico** (Josephine Ormando-2, Gaetano-1) was born on 23 Apr 1919 in Pittston, Luzerne, Pennsylvania. He died on 30 Jun 2009 at the age of 90 in Pittston, Luzerne, Pennsylvania.

Matthew Amadeo Amico and Elide "Elda" Galantini were married on 16 Nov 1946 in Pittston, Luzerne, Pennsylvania. **Elide "Elda" Galantini**, daughter of Ettore Galantini and Maria Stella, was born in Pittston, Luzerne, Pennsylvania.

Matthew Amadeo Amico and Elide Galantini had the following children:

    73   i. **Cataldo "Ky" Amico**
    74   ii. **Elizabeth Amico**
    75   iii. **Matthew Amico**
    76   iv. **Kathleen Amico**
    77   v. **David Amico**

22. **Louis T. Amico** (Josephine Ormando-2, Gaetano-1) was born on 23 Oct 1921 in Pittston, Luzerne, Pennsylvania. He died on 17 Jun 1990 at the age of 68 in Swoyersville, Luzerne, Pennsylvania.

Louis T. Amico and Sara Giunta were married on 29 Nov 1947 in Pittston, Luzerne, Pennsylvania. **Sara Giunta**, daughter of Salvatore Giunta and Grazia Sberna, was born on 28 Apr 1922 in San Cataldo, Caltanissetta, Sicily, Italy. She died on 21 Jul 2011 at the age of 89 in Wilkes-Barre, Luzerne, Pennsylvania.

Louis T. Amico and Sara Giunta had the following children:

    78   i. **Lucille Amico**, born 7 Mar 1950, Luzerne County, Pennsylvania, USA; died 10 Jul 2007, Columbia, Boone, Missouri.
    79   ii. **Thomas Amico**

23. **Anthony Prizzi** (Lucia Ormando-2, Gaetano-1) was born on 12 Sep 1901 in San Cataldo, Caltanissetta, Sicily, Italy. He died in Jan 1972 at the age of 70 in Wyoming, Luzerne, Pennsylvania. He was buried in Jan 1972 at Denison Cemetery in Swoyersville, Luzerne, Pennsylvania.

Anthony Prizzi and Helen Cummings were married on 20 Oct 1934 in Pittston, Luzerne, Pennsylvania. **Helen Cummings**, daughter of Michael Cummings and Catherine Reilly, was born on 9 Sep 1902 in Pittston, Luzerne, Pennsylvania. She died in Jan 1983 at the age of 80 in Scranton, Lackawanna, Pennsylvania.

24. **Anna Prizzi** (Lucia Ormando-2, Gaetano-1) was born on 15 Aug 1904 in Pittston, Luzerne, Pennsylvania. She died on 15 Aug 1976 at the age of 72 in Easton, Northampton, Pennsylvania.

Anna Prizzi and Angelo Occhipenti were married on 10 Aug 1919 in Pittston, Luzerne, Pennsylvania. **Angelo Occhipenti**, son of Salvatore Occhipenti and Francesca Napolitano, was born on 15 Mar 1898 in San Cataldo, Caltanissetta, Sicily, Italy. He died on 30 Jan 1946 at the age of 47 in White Haven, Luzerne, Pennsylvania.

Angelo Occhipenti and Anna Prizzi had the following children:

    80   i. **Frances Lucille Occhipenti**, born 1920, Pittston, Luzerne, Pennsylvania; died 1968, Wyoming, Luzerne, Pennsylvania.
    81   ii. **Lucille Elizabeth Occhipenti**, born 20 Oct 1923, Pittston, Luzerne, Pennsylvania; died 9 May 2007, Pittston, Luzerne, Pennsylvania.

Anna Prizzi and Joseph Franciosa were married in Jan 1953 in Pittston, Luzerne, Pennsylvania. **Joseph Franciosa**, son of Michael Franciosa, was born on 4 Mar 1895 in Volturino, Foggia, Italy. He died on 11 Dec 1973 at the age of 78 in Easton, Northampton, Pennsylvania.

25. **Rosario Calogero "Ross" Prizzi** (Lucia Ormando-2, Gaetano-1) was born on 28 Sep 1906 in San Cataldo, Caltanissetta, Sicily, Italy. He died on 14 May 1996 at the age of 89 in Old Forge, Lackawanna, Pennsylvania.

Rosario Calogero "Ross" Prizzi and Elizabeth A. Biscontini were married on 7 Nov 1934 in Old Forge, Lackawanna, Pennsylvania. **Elizabeth A. Biscontini**, daughter of Giulio Biscontini and Annetta Rossi, was born on 4 Dec 1905 in Old Forge, Lackawanna, Pennsylvania. She died on 31 Jul 1996 at the age of 90 in Old Forge, Lackawanna, Pennsylvania.

Rosario Calogero Prizzi and Elizabeth A. Biscontini had the following children:

    82   i. **Lucille Prizzi**
           ii. **Rosalie Prizzi**

26. **Anthony Ormando** (Giovanni-2, Gaetano-1) was born on 26 Feb 1915 in Pittston, Luzerne, Pennsylvania. He died in 1994 at the age of 79 in Toms River, Ocean, New Jersey.

Anthony Ormando and Josephine Angello were married about 1938 in Pittston, Luzerne, Pennsylvania. **Josephine Angello**, daughter of Joseph Anthony Angello and Maria Marchese, was born on 18 Jul 1916 in Pittston, Luzerne, Pennsylvania. She died on 17 Jan 2003 at the age of 86 in Toms River, Ocean, New Jersey.

Anthony Ormando and Josephine Angello had the following child:

      i. **John Ormando** was born on 21 Jun 1939 in Pittston, Luzerne, Pennsylvania. He died on 30 Dec 2001 at the age of 62 in Toms River, Ocean, New Jersey.

27. **Anthony "Nino" Agati** (Maria Ormando-2, Gaetano-1) was born on 8 Nov 1915 in Pittston, Luzerne, Pennsylvania. He died on 18 May 1990 at the age of 74 in Philadelphia, Pennsylvania, USA.

Anthony "Nino" Agati and Stephanie Volpe were married on 14 Oct 1939 in Pittston, Luzerne, Pennsylvania. **Stephanie Volpe**, daughter of Santo Angelo Volpe and Dorothea Licata, was born on 1 Dec 1916 in Pennsylvania. She died on 3 Nov 2009 at the age of 92 in Harveys Lake, Luzerne, Pennsylvania.

Anthony Agati and Stephanie Volpe had the following children:

      i. **Frank S. Agati** was born on 8 Jun 1941 in Pittston, Luzerne, Pennsylvania. He died on 21 Sep 1967 at the age of 26 in Bethesda, Montgomery, Maryland.
      ii. **Santo A. Agati**
      iii. **Anthony Agati Jr**

28. **Grace Agati** (Maria Ormando-2, Gaetano-1) was born on 21 Nov 1917 in Pittston, Luzerne, Pennsylvania. She died on 25 Oct 2008 at the age of 90 in Pittston, Luzerne, Pennsylvania.

Grace Agati and John Walsh were married on 9 Aug 1947 in Pittston, Luzerne, Pennsylvania. **John Walsh**, son of John Walsh and Mary Finn, was born on 9 Aug 1909 in Exeter, Luzerne, Pennsylvania. John died on 17 Dec 1989 at the age of 80 in Pittston, Luzerne, Pennsylvania.

John Walsh and Grace Agati had the following children:

    83   i. **Jacqueline Walsh**
          ii. **Geraldine Walsh**

Grace Agati and Michael Silver were married about 1975 in Pittston, Luzerne, Pennsylvania. **Michael Silver**, son of Frank Silverio and Philomena "Minnie" Cardone, was born on 3 Jan 1921 in Pittston, Luzerne, Pennsylvania. He died on 22 Jan 2012 at the age of 91 in Pittston, Luzerne, Pennsylvania.

29. **Angelina Agati** (Maria Ormando-2, Gaetano-1) was born on 19 Aug 1919 in Pittston, Luzerne, Pennsylvania. She died on 29 May 1984 at the age of 64 in Wyoming, Luzerne, Pennsylvania.

Angelina Agati and Louis Thomas Costello were married on 2 Sep 1950 in Exeter, Luzerne, Pennsylvania. **Louis Thomas Costello**, son of Carmen Costello and Julia Spinelli, was born on 6 Feb 1923 in West Pittston, Luzerne, Pennsylvania. He died on 2 Dec 2009 at the age of 86 in Scranton, Lackawanna, Pennsylvania.

30. **Guy Angelo Agati** (Maria Ormando-2, Gaetano-1) was born on 23 May 1921 in Pittston, Luzerne, Pennsylvania. He died on 5 Apr 1985 at the age of 63 in Kingston, Luzerne, Pennsylvania.

Guy Angelo Agati and Norma Josephine Zanghi were married in 1950 in Philadelphia, Pennsylvania. **Norma Josephine Zanghi**, daughter of Angelo Zanghi and Genevieve Cartesano, was born on 11 Nov 1929 in Philadelphia, Pennsylvania. She died on 7 Dec 2010 at the age of 81 in Kingston, Luzerne, Pennsylvania.

Guy Angelo Agati and Norma Josephine Zanghi had the following children:

    84   i. **Angela Agati**
    85   ii. **Maria Agati**

31. **Sarah Agati** (Maria Ormando-2, Gaetano-1)

Sarah Agati and David Koch were married on 19 Apr 1947 in West Wyoming, Luzerne, Pennsylvania. **David Koch**, son of John Koch and Florence Rozell, was born in Schenectady, Schenectady, New York.

32. **Josephine Agati** (Maria Ormando-2, Gaetano-1)

Josephine Agati and Theodore James Anderson were married on 19 Apr 1947 in Wyoming, Luzerne, Pennsylvania. **Theodore James Anderson**, son of Fred Anderson and Isabel Saunders, was born on 4 Sep 1924 in West Wyoming, Luzerne, Pennsylvania. He died on 11 Oct 2009 at the age of 85 in Kingston, Luzerne, Pennsylvania.

33. **Joseph L. Bellanca** (Rosina Ormando-2, Gaetano-1) was born on 10 Jul 1914 in Pittston, Luzerne, Pennsylvania. He died on 20 Oct 1994 at the age of 80 in Wilkes-Barre, Luzerne, Pennsylvania.

Joseph L. Bellanca and Julia Kachurak were married on 25 Oct 1941 in Pittston, Luzerne, Pennsylvania. They were divorced on 14 Mar 1947 in Pittston, Luzerne, Pennsylvania. **Julia Kachurak**, daughter of Nicholas Kachurak and Ann Silkovich, was born in 1916 in Passaic, Passaic, New Jersey.

Joseph L. Bellanca and Margaret Neary were married on 28 Aug 1948 in Pittston, Luzerne, Pennsylvania. **Margaret Neary**, daughter of Joseph Neary and Rose Mary Anzik, was born on 14 Nov 1918 in Rosedale, Defiance, Ohio. She died on 6 Feb 2007 at the age of 88 in Pittston, Luzerne, Pennsylvania.

34. **Anthony Angelo Bellanca** (Rosina Ormando-2, Gaetano-1) was born on 2 Dec 1916 in Pittston, Luzerne, Pennsylvania. Anthony died on 16 Jul 1994 at the age of 77 in Wyoming, Luzerne, Pennsylvania.

Anthony Angelo Bellanca and Mary Calabrese were married on 20 Jun 1942 in Pittston, Luzerne, Pennsylvania. **Mary Calabrese**, daughter of Raymond Calabrese and Julia Arcarese, was born on 28 Mar 1917 in New Derry, Westmoreland, Pennsylvania. She died on 27 May 2003 at the age of 86 in Wilkes-Barre, Luzerne, Pennsylvania.

Anthony Angelo Bellanca and Mary Calabrese had the following children:

        i. **Rosina F. Bellanca** was born on 28 Jun 1943 in Pittston, Luzerne, Pennsylvania. She died on 22 Mar 2012 at the age of 68 in Wilkes-Barre, Luzerne, Pennsylvania.
      ii. **Maryann Bellanca**

35. **Stephen L. Bellanca** (Rosina Ormando-2, Gaetano-1) was born on 21 Oct 1918 in Pittston, Luzerne, Pennsylvania. He died on 27 Sep 1998 at the age of 79 in Wilkes-Barre, Luzerne, Pennsylvania.

Stephen L. Bellanca and Nellie DeFrancesco were married on 30 Nov 1946 in Pittston, Luzerne, Pennsylvania. **Nellie DeFrancesco**, daughter of Colegro DeFrancesco and Marie Lovecchio, was born in 1924 in Pittston, Luzerne, Pennsylvania. She died on 23 Apr 1958 at the age of 34 in Exeter, Luzerne, Pennsylvania.

Stephen L. Bellanca and Isabel Argenio were married about 1962 in Pittston, Luzerne, Pennsylvania. **Isabel Argenio**, daughter of Phillip Argenio and Emilia Mirro, was born on 11 Aug 1919 in Pittston, Luzerne, Pennsylvania. She died on 11 May 2010 at the age of 90 in Pittston, Luzerne, Pennsylvania.

36. **Concetta Marie "Connie" Bellanca**

37. **Samuel Bellanca Jr.**

Author's Notes

In the course of my research for this book, I have adhered as closely as possible to the National Genealogical Society's Standards for Sound Genealogical Research. When one encounters the words "possibly," "probably," or "likely" they are the author's conclusions based on the available evidence. I have limited those occurrences to the extent possible.

With regard to dates, when referring to a recurring date, I use the form Month Day. For actual dates, I use the Day Month Year that is standard genealogical practice. With regard to names, I use the subject's Italian given name when introducing them and their Americanized name thereafter. The only exceptions are those instances where the person in question never Americanized their name.

Where a long narrative is quoted, the work is indented and noted at the end of the passage. Otherwise, cited works are in quotes and/or notated appropriately.

For assembling the genealogy of the Ormando family, I used RootsMagic version 6.0 from RootsMagic, Inc. I utilized many sources including Ancestry.com, genealogybank.com, familysearch.org, Luzerne County Library System, and the Luzerne County Historical Society. Since the time that my ancestors immigrated was near the turn of the twentieth century, I also used sources contemporary for the times, including books, newspaper articles, and travel guides.

Please note that for the Descendants of Gaetano Ormando section of the book, birth dates are not provided for those who are living to protect their privacy.

Bibliography

Online Databases

1910 United States Federal Census; population schedule; Digital images. Ancestry.com. http://www.ancestry.com

1920 United States Federal Census; population schedule; Digital images. Ancestry.com. http://www.ancestry.com

1930 United States Federal Census; population schedule; Digital images. Ancestry.com. http://www.ancestry.com

Border Crossings: From Canada to U.S., 1895-1956; Digital images; Ancestry.com; http://www.ancestry.com

California Death Index, 1940-1997; Digital images; Ancestry.com; http://www.ancestry.com

Connecticut Department of Health. Connecticut Death Index, 1949-2001; Digital images; Ancestry.com; http://www.ancestry.com

"District of Columbia Marriages, 1811-1950." Index and images. FamilySearch. https://familysearch.org

Iowa State Census Collection, 1836-1925; ; Digital images; Ancestry.com; http://www.ancestry.com.

Iowa, Births and Christenings Index, 1857-1947; Digital images; Ancestry.com; http://www.ancestry.com

"Italy, Caltanissetta, Caltanissetta, Civil Registration (Tribunale), 1866-1910." Images. State Archive of Caltanissetta (Archivio di Stato di Caltanissetta), Caltanissetta, Italy; http://www.familysearch.org

National Archives and Records Administration. U.S. World War II Army Enlistment Records, 1938-1946; Digital images; Ancestry.com; http://www.ancestry.com

New York Passenger Lists, 1820-1957; Digital images; Ancestry.com; http://www.ancestry.com.

Pennsylvania Veterans Burial Cards, 1777-1999; ; Digital images; Ancestry.com; http://www.ancestry.com.

"Pennsylvania, County Marriages, 1885-1950;" Digital images. FamilySearch. https://familysearch.org.

New York, Marriages, 1686-1980." Index. FamilySearch. https://familysearch.org

Social Security Death Index; Digital images; Ancestry.com; http://www.ancestry.com

"United States, Italians to America Index, 1855-1900," index, FamilySearch; http://www.familysearch.org

U.S. City Directories (Beta); Digital images; Ancestry.com; http://www.ancestry.com

U.S. Naturalization Records - Original Documents, 1795-1972 (World Archives Project); Digital images; Ancestry.com; http://www.ancestry.com

U.S. Passport Applications, 1795-1925; Digital images; Ancestry.com; http://www.ancestry.com

U.S. Public Records Index; Digital images; Ancestry.com; http://www.ancestry.com

U.S. Public Records Index, Volume 2; Digital images; Ancestry.com; http://www.ancestry.com

U.S. Public Records Index; Digital images; Ancestry.com; http://www.ancestry.com

U.S. World War II Draft Registration Cards, 1942; Digital images; Ancestry.com; http://www.ancestry.com

U.S., Department of Veterans Affairs BIRLS Death File, 1850-2010; Digital images; Ancestry.com; http://www.ancestry.com

United States Obituary Collection; Digital images; Ancestry.com; http://www.ancestry.com

World War I Draft Registration Cards, 1917-1918; Digital images; Ancestry.com; http://www.ancestry.com

Periodicals

Cosidine, Bob. "On the Line." *Anderson Herald Bulletin* (Anderson, IN), March 25, 1960, A36.

Hinton, Harold B.; "Opposition Forms to Neutrality Bill." *New York Times* (1923-Current File), Jun 17, 1939, Page 1.

Hughey, Bud. "Tony and 'The Great One'..A Story of Pals." *The Geneva Times* (Lake Geneva, NY), January 1962, A5.

Hunt, Thomas, and Tona, Michael A., "Men of Montedoro." *Informer - History of American Crime and Law Enforcement* (Middlebury, VT), no. 3 (2011): 5-31.

Kashatus, William C. "White Haven Center Brings Decades of Experience." *The Citizen's Voice* (Wilkes-Barre, PA), June 10, 2010, C1.

Oliver, Sir Thomas. "The Sulphur Miners of Sicily: Their Work, Diseases, and Accident Insurance." British Medical Journal 2, no. 2635 (July 1, 1911): 12-14.

Rosenthal, Am; "Russia Accuses Us of Seeking Delay on Disarmament." *New York Times (1923-Current File)*, Jan 10, 1947, Page 1.

Selden, Charles A.; "Peace Conference Defers its Vacation." *New York Times (1857-1922)*, Aug 11, 1919, Page 1.

Special to The New York Times. "Strikers Expect Short Suspension." *New York Times (1923-Current File)*, Sep 04, 1923, Page 19.

———. "Andrew Carnegie Dies of Pneumonia in His 84th Year." *New York Times (1857-1922)*, Aug 12, 1919, Page 1.

———. "Hard Coal Miners show Peace is Sure." *New York Times (1857-1922)*, Sep 07 1922, Page 3.

———. "Four Miners' Houses Dynamited in Pittston." *New York Times (1923-Current File)*, Jul 14, 1923, Page 5.

———. "Our Red Cross Gave Aid Throughout World in War." *New York Times (1923-Current File)*, Jan 12, 1947, Page 1.

———. "Radicals in Power as Miners Convene." *New York Times (1923-Current File)*, Jun 27, 1923, Page 30.

———. "Coal Miners Gather to Frame Demands." *New York Times (1923-Current File)*, Jun 29, 1925, Page 1.

———. "Mine Union Leaders are Slain in Feud." *New York Times (1923-Current File)*, Feb 17, 1928, Page 23.

———. "Mine Union Leader Guilty of Killing." *New York Times (1923-Current File)*, Apr 15, 1928, Page 50.

Staff Reporters. "Veterans Will Renew Friendship on Scene of Southern Battles." *Sunday Independent* (Wilkes-Barre, PA), September 14, 1913, Page 1.

———. "Pittston," *Sunday Independent* (Wilkes-Barre, PA), September 14, 1913; Page 16

———. "18 Injured in Panic on Trolley," *Sunday Independent* (Wilkes-Barre, PA), August 14, 1919, Page 1.

———. "Shipload of Refugees is Docked at Antwerp," *Sunday Independent* (Wilkes-Barre, PA), June 18, 1939; Page 1

———. "St. Rocco's Picnic Plans Progressing," *Sunday Independent* (Wilkes-Barre, PA), June 18, 1939; Page C – 5.

———. "Death Claims Cataldo Amico." August 10, 1961, Evening edition, sec. A.

Staff Reporters. "Big War Force First," *The Washington Post* (Washington, DC) September 20, 1913, Page 1.

Staff Reporters. "Daystrom Opens Defense Exhibit at Elizabeth," *The Westfield Leader* (Westfield, NJ), March 6, 1952. Page 24.

Staff Reporters. "District Organizer Slain in Cappellini's Office," *The Wilkes-Barre Record* (Wilkes-Barre, PA), 23 February 1928, Page 1.

Staff Reporters. "Italian Club Charter Granted by Court," *Wilkes-Barre Times-Leader* (Wilkes-Barre, PA), July 29, 1915, Page 15.

Washington, Booker T. "The Man Farthest Down – Child Labor and the Sulphur Mines." The Outlook XCVIII (September 1911): 342-49.

Books

Abbott, Grace; *The Immigrant and the Community*; New York, The Century Company; 1917.

Adir, Karin; *The Great Clowns of American Television*. Jefferson, NC; McFarland Classics, 1988.

Alexander, June Granatir; *Daily Life in Immigrant America, 1870-1920*. Rev. ed. Chicago, IL: Ivan R. Dee, 2009.

Astarita, Tommaso; *Between Salt Water and Holy Water*. New York, NY: W.W. Norton & Company, 2006.

Baedeker, Karl; *Italy: Handbook for Travelers*. Leipzig, Germany: Karl Baedeker, 1903.

Boldt, Julius; *Trachoma*. London, England: Hodder and Stoughton, 1904

Brandenburg, Broughton; *Imported Americans: The Story of the Experiences of a Disguised American and his Wife*; New York; Frederick A. Stokes Company; 1904.

Cannato, Vincent J., American Passage. New York, NY: Harper Collins, 2009.

Clark, Francis E; *Our Italian Fellow Citizens: In Their Old Homes and Their New;* Boston, MA; Small, Maynard, & Company; 1919.

Cross, Peter Morton. *Ellis Island Interviews: In Their Own Words*. New York, NY: Facts On File, 1997.

Daniels, Roger. Coming to America. New York, NY: Visual Education Corporation, 2002.

Davis, Michael M. *Immigrant Health and the Community*. New York, NY: Harper & Brothers, 1921.

Foerster, Robert; *The Italian Immigrant of Our Times*; Boston, MA: Harvard University Press, 1919.

Holmes, George; *The Oxford History of Italy*; Oxford, Great Britain: Oxford University Press, 1997.

Laskin, David; *The Long Way Home: An American Journey from Ellis Island to the Great War*; New York, NY: Harper Collins, 2010.

Lord, Elliot, Trenor, John, and Barrows, Samuel; *The Italian in America*; New York; B.F. Buck & Company; 1905.

Mangano, Antonio; *Sons of Italy: A Social and Religious Study of the Italians in America;* New York, NY; Missionary Education Movement; 1917.

Marble, John Emerson; *History of Luzerne, Lackawanna, and Wyoming Counties, PA*; New York, W. W. Munsell & Company; 1880.

Paton, William Agnew; *Picturesque Sicily*; New York; Harper and Brothers; 1897.

Pozzetta, George; *Italian Americans*; Gale Encyclopedia of Multicultural America;. 2000; Encyclopedia.com. (March 7, 2013).
http://www.encyclopedia.com/doc/1G2-3405800092.html

Rose, Phillip; *The Italians in America*; New York; George H. Doran Company; 1922.

Sartorio, Enrico C; *Social and Religious Life of Italians in America*; Boston, MA; Christopher Publishing House; 1918.

Von Drehle, David; *Triangle: The Fire That Changed America*; New York; Grove Press; 2003.

Web sites, e-sources

Civic Heraldry, Araldicacivica;
http://www.araldicacivica.it/pdf/decreti%20citta/cl/sancataldo.pdf; accessed 12 Oct 2012.

Demetri, Justin. "The Early Struggles of Italians in America." Life in Italy. Last modified October 5, 2009. Accessed November 21, 2012. http://www.lifeinitaly.com/heritage/italian-discrimination.

Euro Events and Travel, LLC, ed. "Italian Wedding Traditions." WorldWeddingTraditions.com. Last modified 2004. Accessed November 27, 2012. http://worldweddingtraditions.com/locations/west_europe_traditions/italian_traditions.html.

Gale Group. "The Cost of Being Sick." Encyclopedia.com. Last modified 2001. Accessed February 26, 2013. http://www.encyclopedia.com/doc/ 1G2-3468301282.html.

———. "The Depression and Education." Encyclopedia.com. Last modified 2001. Accessed February 26, 2013. http://www.encyclopedia.com/doc/1G2-3468301123.html.

———. "Women Go to Work." Encyclopedia.com. Last modified 2001. Accessed February 26, 2013. http://www.encyclopedia.com/doc/1G2-3468300895.html.

———. "The Wonder Drugs: 'Magic Bullets' Against Disease." Encyclopedia.com. Last modified 2001. Accessed February 26, 2013. http://www.encyclopedia.com/doc/1G2-3468301646.html.

———. "The Great White Plague'—Tuberculosis Before the Age of Antibiotics.'" Encyclopedia.com. Last modified 2001. Accessed February 26, 2013. http://www.encyclopedia.com/doc/1G2-3468301286.html.

———. "Maternal Mortality—Why Mothers Died." Encyclopedia.com; Last modified 2001. Accessed February 26, 2013; http://www.encyclopedia.com/doc/1G2-3468301289.html.

———. "The 1940s: Medicine and Health: Overview;" Encyclopedia.com. Last modified 2001. Accessed February 26, 2013. http://www.encyclopedia.com/doc/1G2-3468301630.html

———. "The 1930s: Medicine And Health: Overview." Encyclopedia.com. Last modified 2001. Accessed February 26, 2013. http://www.encyclopedia.com/doc/1G2-3468301278.html.

———. "Working Women in the 1930s." Encyclopedia.com. Last modified 2001. Accessed February 26, 2013. http://www.encyclopedia.com/topic/Working_women.aspx#1-1G2:3468301237.htm

HHS, ed. "Life in 1918." The Great Pandemic. Last modified November 11, 2012. Accessed November 27, 2012. http://www.flu.gov/pandemic/history/1918/life_in_1918/health/index.htm.

JRank. "Mortality, Childbirth." Encyclopedia of Death and Dying. Last modified 2013. Accessed February 26, 2013. http://www.deathreference.com/Me-Nu/Mortality-Childbirth.html.

Kenyon College. "History of penicillin." *MicrobeWiki, the student-edited microbiology resource*. Last modified May 2012. Accessed February 26, 2013. http://microbewiki.kenyon.edu/index.php/History_of_penicillin.

Luzerne County, ed. "History of Luzerne County." Luzerne County Living. Last modified October 15, 2012. Accessed November 20, 2012. http://www.luzernecounty.org/living/history_of_luzerne_county.

Merriam-Webster.com; Merriam-Webster, 2011; http://www.merriam-webster.com/

Rapczynski, Joan. "The Italian Immigrant Experience in America (1870-1920)." Yale-New Haven Teachers Institute. Last modified 2012. Accessed November 21, 2012. http://www.yale.edu/ynhti/curriculum/units/1999/3/99.03.06.x.html

Saint Rocco Society of Potenza; "Who is Saint Rocco?" Xtreme Graphics Design; http://www.stroccosociety.com/story1.htm; 12 October 2012.

Saverino, Joan, Ph.D. "Exploring Diversity in Pennsylvania History." Rural Roads, City Streets: Italians in Pennsylvania Student Reading. Last modified 2012. Accessed November 21, 2012. http://www.academia.edu/315025/ITALIAN_IMMIGRANT_FAMILY_PORTRAITS.

Snyder, Thomas; 120 Years of American Education: A Statistical Portrait; National Center for Education Statistics; Publication Number - NCES 93442; January 1993; http://0-nces.ed.gov.opac.acc.msmc.edu/pubs93/93442.pdf; Accessed 6 March 2013

Wikipedia; "Chiesa madre (San Cataldo) --- Wikipedia, L'enciclopedia libera," 2013; http://it.wikipedia.org/w/index.php?title=Chiesa_madre_(San_Cataldo)&oldid=56521534; Online; 4 March2013

Wikipedia; "Infective endocarditis." (2013, April 10). Retrieved 02:39, April 14, 2013, from http://en.wikipedia.org/w/index.php?title=Infective_endocarditis&oldid=549633414

Unpublished Sources

Maziarz, Lucille. Interview by Martin Novak. November 10, 2012.

Novak, Virginia Leonardi. Interview by the author. 2005.

Prizzi, Rosalie. Letter to the author, "Family History," September 21, 2012.

Vital Records

Certificate of Death for Cataldo Giannone, 17 September 1919, File Number 7039677, Commonwealth of Pennsylvania, Department of Health, Bureau of Vital Statistics.

Certificate of Death for Grace DiLorenzo, 27 January 1942, File Number 5197, Commonwealth of Pennsylvania, Department of Health, Bureau of Vital Statistics.

Certificate of Death for Grace Ormando, 19 March 1942, File Number 27766, Commonwealth of Pennsylvania, Department of Health, Bureau of Vital Statistics.

Certificate of Death for Angelo DiLorenzo, 6 November 1942, File Number 99249, Commonwealth of Pennsylvania, Department of Health, Bureau of Vital Statistics.

Certificate of Death for Mary Maloney, 29 October 1943, File Number 30852, Commonwealth of Pennsylvania, Department of Health, Bureau of Vital Statistics.

Certificate of Death for Salvatore Prizzi, 5 April 1952, File Number 6930938, Commonwealth of Pennsylvania, Department of Health, Bureau of Vital Statistics.

Certificate of Death for Angelo Occhipenti, 30 January 1940, File Number 7039678, Commonwealth of Pennsylvania, Department of Health, Bureau of Vital Statistics.

Legal Sources

153 Cong. Rec. S13584 (daily ed. May 23, 2007) (statement of Sen. Menendez). Accessed May 29, 2013. http://books.google.com/

Committee on Immigration, Emigrant Conditions in Europe, Rep. No. 61-748, 3d Sess., at 209 (1910)

Acknowledgements

I wish to thank all of the members of the Ormando family, who provided their insights, and family stories. I especially thank Vince Aquilina for his encouragement and support throughout this project. I am grateful to my mother, Virginia Novak for her assistance in proof reading the many drafts of this work. When writing, it is far too easy to miss the forest for the trees. Having someone who will provide honest feedback, and make the final work better in the process is a blessing.

There have been numerous people along the way who have provided me encouragement and assistance in this work, including Michael Hunt, Editor of *The Informer*; Amanda C. Fontenova, Chief Librarian for the *Luzerne County Historical Society*; Mike Cutillo, Executive Editor of the *Finger Lakes Times*; and the staff at the *Osterhout Free Library* in Wilkes-Barré, Pennsylvania.

Finally, I wish to express my gratitude to my wife Debra for her patience, understanding, and encouragement during my many trips to the Pittston area to do research and the many hours writing this work.

Table of Figures

Unless otherwise noted below, photographs in the text are from the author's private collection or are in the public domain.

1 - Gaetano and Mary Ormando Leonardi at their home at 225 S. Main Street in Pittston, Pennsylvania, circa 1965 3

2 - Map of Sicily, with location of San Cataldo circled. (William Agnew Paton, 1897) 5

3- Gaetano Ormando, patriarch of the Ormando family, circa 1906. Courtesy of Vince Aquilina. 10

4 - The Ormando siblings that came to America, from left – John, Rose, Josephine, Lucy, Maria, and Joseph. Circa 1942. Courtesy of Vince Aquilina 13

5 - Arriving at Ellis Island. Library Of Congress, Prints And Photographs Division 17

6 - Map of Luzerne, Lackawanna, and Wyoming Counties, circa 1880 22

7 - Pittston, circa 1907. Library of Congress, Prints and Photographs Division 25

8 - Section of Pittston, 11th Ward, circa 1930 - Highlighted are 5 West Oak Street, home of Joseph Ormando; 18 Price Street, home of Cataldo Amico; and Saint Rocco's Church Courtesy of The Luzerne County Historical Society 26

9 - Sam Prizzi, one of the founding members of the San Cataldo Society. Courtesy of Rosalie Prizzi. 41

10 - Pittston Depot for the Laurel Line, circa 1910. Courtesy of the Luzerne County Historical Society. 48

11 - Librettos from operas attended by Gaetano and Mary Ormando Leonardi 50

12 - "The Ladies." Grace Ormando DiLorenzo is first on the left. Mary Ormando Leonardi is fourth from the right. 53

13 - Tony Ormando and Mollie DePascale's wedding party, 10 September 1937 Courtesy of Sylvia Ormando. 55

14 - Saint Rocco's Church, circa 1927. Courtesy of The Luzerne County Historical Society... 58

15 - The Amico family, from left – Nellie, Josephine, Grace, Cataldo, Tony, and Sam. Circa 1912. Courtesy of Vince Aquilina 62

16 - Cataldo and Nellie Giannone with their son, Sam, circa 1916. Courtesy of Vince Aquilina. 63

17 - Nellie and Michele Aquilina, circa 1924. Courtesy of Vince Aquilina 64

18 - Michele Aquilina's headstone in St. John's Cemetery 65

19 - Nellie Amico's headstone in Denison Cemetery 65

20 - Angelo Occhipenti and his daughter Frances. 66

21 - Angelo Occhipenti's headstone in Denison Cemetery 67

22 - Anna Prizzi's headstone also in Denison Cemetery 67

23 - Stephen Bellanca and his mother, Rose Ormando Bellanca 68

24 - Nellie Bellanca's Cemetery Monument 70
25- Stephen Bellanca's Cemetery Marker 70
26 - Rosario "Ross" Calogero Prizzi 71
27 - The Amico brothers, from left Louis, Tony, Joseph, Sam (seated), and Matthew. Courtesy of Vince Aquilina 73
28 - Tony Amico during on of his two tours of duty with the U.S. Army. Courtesy of Vince Aquilina. 74
29 - Concetto "Frank" Agati 76
30 - Mary DiLorenzo, circa 1936 80
31 - Bill Maloney and Mary DiLorenzo on their wedding day, 16 June 1939 81
32 - DiLorenzo family monument in Saint Rocco's Cemetery 83
33 - Catal Ormando, circa 1943 84
34 - Lucille Leonardi 87
35 - Edward "Pier" Maziarz 88
36 - Warning sign outside of the abandoned town of Centralia, Pennsylvania (public domain) 93
37 - An empty street in the ghost town of Centralia. 94
38 - The author with his cousin Helen O'Connor, 30 June 1962 97

Index

A

Amico family, 65
Ellis Island, 16
Economic Conditions of Southern Italy, 7
Health Care, 34
Economic Conditions of Southern Italy, 7
Economic Conditions of Southern Italy, 7, 59
Angelo DeLorenzo, 52, 83
Angelo Occhipenti, 66, 67, 130
Ann Prizzi, 66
Anna Kerchanin, 85

B

Bellanca family, 69
Bill Maloney, 80, 81, 82
Italian trick taking card games, 46
Pittston Area Townships and Villages, 24

C

Caltanissetta, 4, 123, 139
Carmela Ormando, 52
Catal Ormando, 84
Cataldo Amico, 18, 29, 65, 71
Cataldo Giannone, 62, 130
Coal Mining Companies, 29, 67, 78
Prejudice, 36
Pittston Area Townships and Villages, 24

D

Prejudice, 36
Delaware, Lackawanna, and Western Railroad, 19
Dennison Cemetery, 67

E

Edward Maziarz, 88
Elizabeth Biscontini, 71
Ellis Island, 15, 16, 17, 18, 57, 64
Sacco and Vanzetti, 37
Pittston Area Townships and Villages, 24, 69

F

Frank Agati, 18, 29, 76, 78

G

Gaetano Leonardi, 2, 32, 42, 52, 53
Gaetano Ormando, 10, 17, 18, 76, 122, 139
Geisinger Hospital, 98
Giuseppe Garibaldi, 51
Grace DeLorenzo, 52, 82
Grace Grifasi, 19, 55
Grace Occhipenti, 10, 18, 76

H

Pittston Area Townships and Villages, 24

I

Italian language newspapers, 45
Italian language newspapers, 45
Italy, 4, 7, 8, 9, 10, 11, 15, 18, 28, 34, 37, 38, 45, 49, 55, 56, 57, 59, 77, 123, 126, 127, 139

J

Jackie Gleason, 73, 75
John L. Lewis, 31
John Ormando, 19, 29
Joseph Ormando, 18, 19, 29, 39, 52, 53, 55
Josephine Ormando, 18

L

La Bohème, 49
Italian language newspapers, 45
Italian language newspapers, 45
Laurel Line, 19, 47, 48, 49
Lucille Leonardi, 87
Luzerne County, 21, 22, 56, 57, 85, 89, 95, 122, 129

M

Mary DeLorenzo, 80, 81
Michele Aquilina, 63, 64, 65

N

Nellie Amico, 62
Nellie Bellanca, 69

O

Ormando family, 8, 10, 11, 18, 19, 21, 24, 25, 28, 32, 38, 39, 42, 47, 48, 50, 52, 54, 55, 56, 57, 58, 59, 71, 87, 95, 97, 98, 122

P

Pittston, 2, 18, 19, 24, 25, 42, 43, 45, 46, 47, 48, 52, 53, 58, 60, 62, 64, 66, 68, 69, 71, 73, 77, 78, 80, 81, 84, 88, 89, 97, 98, 125, 130

Pittston Area Townships and Villages, 24
Prizzi family, 71

R

Cataldo Amico, 18, 62, 63, 65, 73
Rocky Glen, 48, 57, 72
Roman Catholic Church, 58
Rose DeLorenzo, 82
Rose Keating, 84, 85
Rose Ormando, 18, 19
Ross Prizzi, 71
Russ Andolora, 72

S

Sacco and Vanzetti, 37
San Cataldo, 9
Saint Rocco, 58, 59, 60, 78, 89
Saint Rocco's Italian Catholic Church, 58, 59, 60
Saint Rocco's Society, 58
Sam Bellanca, 19, 29, 68
Sam Bonita, 78
San Cataldo, 4, 8, 9, 42, 62, 66, 71, 76, 84
Benevolent Societies, 42
Sara Pilato, 19
bella figura, 53
Scranton, 19, 24, 47, 48, 58, 72
Pittston Area Townships and Villages, 24
Benevolent Societies, 42, 43
Serradifalco`, 66
Tony Amico, 74
Sicily, 4, 7, 11, 15, 19, 21, 33, 51, 59, 84, 95
Sinibaldo Fanti, 57
St. John's Cemetery, 65
Stephen Bellanca, 68

T

Nellie Bellanca, 69
The Mother Church, 8, 9
Tony Amico, 73, 74, 75
Tony Ormando, 33
Transition generation, 10, 47, 51, 55
Angelo Occhipent, 67
Italian trick taking card games, 46
Health Care, 34, 67

U

United Mine Workers, 78

W

Wilkes-Barre, 24, 47, 48, 72, 78, 85, 86, 89, 125
World War I, 8, 46, 49, 69, 74, 88, 123, 124
Wyoming Valley, 21, 22, 23, 24, 29, 42, 45, 47, 48, 49, 58, 72, 95

Y

Pittston Area Townships and Villages, 24

Endnotes

[1] *Araldicacivica*, Civic Heraldry, http://www.araldicacivica.it/pdf/decreti%20citta/cl/sancataldo.pdf
Chapter 1 - Sicily

[2] Karl Baedeker. *Italy: Handbook for Travelers* [Leipzig, Charles Scribner's Sons, 1903], 216.

[3] Il Mezzogiorno – Literally, "midday." It is the traditional Italian term for all of Southern Italy, including Sicily.

[4] Lantifondi is a large agricultural land, usually poorly cultivated and used in extensive crops often alternating pasture.

[5] Eliot Lord. *The Italian in America* [New York, B.F Buck & Company, 1905], page 47.

[6] Philip M. Rose. *The Italians In America*; [New York, George H. Doran Company, 1922], page 43.

[7] Contributori di Wikipedia, "Chiesa madre (San Cataldo)",Wikipedia, L'enciclopedia libera, //it.wikipedia.org/w/index.php?title=Chiesa_madre_(San_Cataldo)&oldid=56521534 (in data 4 marzo 2013).

[8] Ibid

[9] June Granatir Alexander. *Daily Life in Immigrant America: 1870 - 1920* [Chicago, Dee, 2009], 200.

[10] "Italy, Caltanissetta, Serradifalco, Civil Registration (Tribunale), 1866-1910." Images.FamilySearch. Entry for Gaetano Ormando and Grazia Occhipenti married 3 August 1873. Citing Matrimoni (1866 – 1880); digital folder – image 532 of 1,122 images; Record number 80.

[1] Francis E, Clark. *Our Italian Fellow Citizens - In Their Old Homes And Their New* [Boston; Small, Maynard & Company Publishers; 1919], 93.

[2] Trachoma is caused by infection with the bacteria Chlamydia trachomatis. Today it more commonly referred to as granular conjunctivitis.

[3] Julius Boldt. *Trachoma* [London, Hodder and Stoughton; 1904], page 142

[4] Grace Abbott; The Immigrant and the Community; [New York, The Century Company, 1917], page 141.

[5] Ben Morreale and Robert Carola, *Italian Americans: The immigrant experience* [S.I., Hugh Lauter Levin Associates, 2000], 99.

[6] 1910 United States Federal Census, population schedule, Pittston, Luzerne, Pennsylvania, Enumeration District [ED] 096, sheet 7A, dwelling 106, family 114, Cataldo Amico household; National Archives microfilm publication T624, roll 1368; digital image, Ancestry.com, http://www.ancestry.com; accessed 13 Nov 2012.

[7] Cataldo Amico, Petition for Naturalization, Page 167 of 464, Petition Number 3261, Luzerne, Pennsylvania, Middle District of Pennsylvania, District Court; Naturalization Records, 1795 – 1972; Digital Image; Ancestry.com. http://www.ancestry.com; 2010.

[8] List or Manifest of Alien Passengers for the United States arriving in New York from Palermo, Italy; 11 March 1903, on the Trojan Prince, page 17/list 2, line number 29, Salvatore Prizzi, the record confirming his Italian origin, last residence in San Cataldo, Digital Image; accessed in "New York Passenger Lists;" online at Ancestry.com, 10 November 2012.

[9] List or Manifest of Alien Passengers for the United States arriving in New York from Palermo, Italy; 9 July 1903, on the Citta Di Napoli; page 23/list 3, line numbers 6, 7, 9 and 10; for Giuseppa Ormando, Calogera Amico, Lucia Ormando, and Gaetano Prizzi; the record confirming their Italian origin; last residence in San Cataldo; accessed in "New York Passenger Lists;" online at Ancestry.com, 10 November 2012.

[10] List or Manifest of Alien Passengers for the United States arriving in New York from Palermo, Italy; 27 March 1904, on the Citta Di Milano. Page 25/list S, line numbers 27 and 28, for Giuseppie Ormando, Giovanni Ormando; the record confirming their Italian origin, last residence in San Cataldo, accessed in "New York Passenger Lists;" online at Ancestry.com, 10 November 2012.

[11] List or Manifest of Alien Passengers for the United States arriving in New York from Palermo, Italy; 24 March 1907, on the Sofia Hohenberg. Page 90/list number 29, line number 28, for Concetto Agati; the record confirming his Italian origin, last residence in San Cataldo, accessed in "New York Passenger Lists;" online at Ancestry.com, 10 November 2012.

[12] List or Manifest of Alien Passengers for the United States arriving in New York from Palermo, Italy; 22 July 1909, on the Principe Di Piemonte. Page 190/list number 206, line numbers 13 – 16, for Lucia Ormando, Gaetano Prizzi, Anna Prizzi, and Ross Prizzi; the record confirming their Italian origin, last residence in San Cataldo, accessed in "New York Passenger Lists;" online at Ancestry.com, 10 November 2012.

[13] List or Manifest of Alien Passengers for the United States arriving in New York from Palermo, Italy; 19 August 1909, on the Regina d'Italia. Page 49/list number 205, line numbers 8 – 12, for Gaetano Ormando, Grace Occhipenti, Maria Ormando, and Rosina Ormando; the record confirming their Italian origin, last residence in San Cataldo, accessed in "New York Passenger Lists;" online at Ancestry.com, 10 November 2012.

[14] List or Manifest of Alien Passengers for the United States arriving in New York from Palermo, Italy; 30 Mar 1911, on the Venezia. List number 50, line numbers 12 and 13, for Giovanni Ormando, and Rosaria Pilato; the record confirming their Italian origin, last residence in San Cataldo, accessed in "New York Passenger Lists;" online at Ancestry.com, November 2012.

[15] List or Manifest of Alien Passengers for the United States arriving in New York from Palermo, Italy; 13 Apr 1911, on the Sant' Anna. List number 58, line number 24, for Giovanni Ormando; the record confirming his Italian origin, last residence in San Cataldo, accessed in "New York Passenger Lists;" online at Ancestry.com, November 2012.

[16] List or Manifest of Alien Passengers for the United States arriving in New York from Palermo, Italy; 23 Feb 1913, on the Canada. List number 37, line number 23, for Rosaria Pilato; the record confirming her Italian origin, last residence in San Cataldo, accessed in "New York Passenger Lists;" online at Ancestry.com, November 2012.

[17] Alphabetical Manifest Cards of Alien Arrivals at Vanceboro, Maine, ca. 1906-December 24, 1952; 9 Jul 1913, Record for Joseph Ormando and Rosaria Pilato; the record confirming their Italian origin, legal residence at 5 West Oak Street, Pittston, Pennsylvania, accessed in "Border Crossings: From Canada to U.S., 1895-1954;" online at Ancestry.com, November 2012.

[18] List or Manifest of Alien Passengers for the United States arriving in New York from Palermo, Italy; 24 Oct 1913, on the San Guglielmo. List number 83, line number 06, for Salvatore Bellanca; the record confirming his Italian origin, last residence in San

Cataldo, accessed in "New York Passenger Lists;" online at Ancestry.com, November 2012.

[19] List or Manifest of Alien Passengers for the United States arriving in New York from Palermo, Italy; 11 July 1914, on the Sant' Anna. List number 91, line numbers 3 – 7, for Grazia Grifasi Ormando, Grazia Ormando, Maria Ormando, Gaetano Ormando, and Cataldo Ormando; the record confirming their Italian origin, last residence in San Cataldo, accessed in "New York Passenger Lists;" online at Ancestry.com, November 2012.

[20] Wikipedia contributors, "Lackawanna and Wyoming Valley Railroad," Wikipedia, The Free Encyclopedia, http://en.wikipedia.org/w/index.php?title=Lackawanna_and_Wyoming_Valley_Railroad&oldid=524613591 (accessed March 4, 2013).

Chapter 3 – Where They Lived

[21] Luzerne County, ed. "History of Luzerne County." Luzerne County Living. Last modified October 15, 2012. Accessed November 20, 2012. http://www.luzernecounty.org/living/history_of_luzerne_county.

[22] Marble, Page 68.

[23] Ibid, Page 68.

[24] Ibid, Page 84.

[25] Ibid, Page 88.

[26] Ibid, Page 332.

[27] U.S. City Directories, 1821 – 1989 (Beta); Pittston, Pennsylvania; City Directory (1915); Digital Image; Image 8 of 312; Ancestry.com; http://www.ancestry.com ; Accessed 4 March 2013

Chapter 4 – Challenges They Faced

[1] A boy employed in a coal breaker to pick slate from coal

[2] Cataldo Amico, Petition for Naturalization, Page 167 of 464; Frank listed his occupation as stonemason; Ancestry.com; http://www.ancestry.com; Accessed 4 March 2013

3 An underground coal mine is referred to as a colliery in Great Britain.

[4] Inkerman is a community within the Jenkins Township in Luzerne County, Pennsylvania.

[5] World War II draft registration card for John Ormando; 24 April 1942; Philadephia, Pennsylvania; Local Board Number 78; Digital Image; Image Number 1363 of 3205; Ancestry.com; http://www.ancestry.com; 2012.

[6] World War I draft registration card for Sam Bellanca; 15 June 1917; Pittston, Pennsylvania; National archives microfilm M1509; Roll Number 1893746; Ancestry.com; http://www.ancestry.com; 2012.

[7] "*Death Claims Cataldo Amico*," The Times Leader (Wilkes-Barre, PA), August 10, 1961, Evening edition, sec. A,

[8] Alexander, pages 114-115.

[9] Antonio Mangano; *Sons of Italy: A Social And Religious Study Of The Italians In America*; Missionary Education Movement of the United States and Canada; New York; 1917; Page 27.

[10] Thomas Snyder; *120 Years of American Education: A Statistical Portrait*; National Center for Education Statistics; Publication Number - NCES 93442; January 1993; http://0-nces.ed.gov.opac.acc.msmc.edu/pubs93/93442.pdf; Accessed 6 March 2013.

[11] Alexander, page 215-216.

[12] United States Department of Health and Human Services; *Life in 1918*; Retrieved from The Great Pandemic: http://www.flu.gov/pandemic/history/1918/life_in_1918/health/index.htm; accessed 11 Nov 2012.

[13] "*Maternal Mortality—Why Mothers Died.*" American Decades. 2001. Encyclopedia.com. (March 13, 2013). http://www.encyclopedia.com/doc/1G2-3468301289.html

[14] Grace Abbott. The Immigrant and the Community; [New York, The Century Company, 1917], page 153.

[15] Ibid, page 153.

[16] *Predjudice*; Merriam-Webster.com; Merriam-Webster, 2011; http://www.merriam-webster.com/dictionary/prejudice; Accessed 6 March 2013.

[17] *Discrimination*; Merriam-Webster.com; Merriam-Webster, 2011; http://www.merriam-webster.com/dictionary/discrimination; Accessed 6 March 2013.

[18] *Emigration Conditions in Europe*. Reports of the U.S. Immigration Commission [Washington, DC, U.S. Government Printing Office, 1911], Page 209

[19] Morreale, & Carola, 150.

[20] 153 Cong. Rec. S13584 (daily ed. May 23, 2007) (statement of Sen. Menendez). Accessed May 29, 2013. http://books.google.com/.

[21] Ibid, page S13584

[22] A Mafia-like, criminal organization that uses political patronage to protect its interests.

[23] Explore PA History; *Pennsylvania and the Great Depression*; http://explorepahistory.com/story.php?storyId=1-9-1B; retrieved 21 November 2012

[24] "*Making do: Family Life in the Depression.*" American Decades. 2001. Encyclopedia.com. (March 13, 2013). http://www.encyclopedia.com/doc/1G2-3468301233.html

Chapter 5 – How They Lived

[1] Alexander, 195.

[2] "San Cataldo Society to Dedicate Home," *Sunday Independent*, Wilkes-Barre, 24 September 1939.

[3] "San Cataldo Society Completes Program For Dedication," *Sunday Independent*, Wilkes-Barre, 8 October 1939.

[4] 1910 U.S. Federal Census, Pittston City, Luzerne, Pennsylvania, ED 96, Sheet 7A, Dwelling 106, Family 114, Cataldo Amico (spelled incorrectly in the census as Ameska Cataldia) household, digital image, Ancestry.com. http://www.ancestry.com; accessed November 2012.

[5] 1930 U.S. Federal Census, Pittston, Luzerne, Pennsylvania, ED 40-168, Sheet 10A, Dwelling 161, Family Number 167, Cataldo Amico household, digital image, Ancestry.com. http://www.ancestry.com; accessed November 2012.

[6] 1930 U.S. Federal Census, Pittston, Luzerne, Pennsylvania, ED 40-168, Sheet 12B, Dwelling 196, Family Number 208, Giuseppe Ormando household, digital image, Ancestry.com. http://www.ancestry.com; accessed November 2012.

[7] Alexander, 167.

[8] Wikipedia contributors, "Lackawanna and Wyoming Valley Railroad," Wikipedia, The Free Encyclopedia, http://en.wikipedia.org/w/index.php?title=Lackawanna_and_Wyoming_Valley_Railroad&oldid=524613591 (accessed March 4, 2013).

[9] La bohème; In Wikipedia, The Free Encyclopedia. Retrieved 22:35, December 1, 2012, from http://en.wikipedia.org/w/index.php?title=La_boh%C3%A8me&oldid=525801125

Chapter 6 – The Family at Home

[1] Interview with Rose DiLorenzo Maloney by the author, August 2012.

[2] "United States, Italians to America Index, 1855-1900," index, FamilySearch (https://familysearch.org/pal:/MM9.1.1/KD4T-3KV : accessed 25 Mar 2013), Fante Sinibaldo, 1900.

[3] "United States Census, 1930," index and images, FamilySearch (https://familysearch.org/pal:/MM9.1.1/XH77-BSD : accessed 25 Mar 2013), Sinabaldo Fanti, 1930.

[4] Pennsylvania Department of Health; Online Death Indices; 1906 – 1962, Death Index record for Sinibaldo Fanti, Year: 1946. File Number 87619. File Name: D-46 E-G.pdf. Page 96 of 252.

Chapter 7 – Biographical Vignettes

[1] "Italy, Caltanissetta, Caltanissetta, Civil Registration (Tribunale), 1866-1910." Images.FamilySearch. Entry for Calogera Amico, born 22 September 1898. Citing Nati (1881 – 1890); digital folder – image 2,419 of 3,111 images; Record number 637.

[2] Nellie's brothers Joseph, Matthew and Louis were all born after her marriage to Cataldo Giannone.

[3] "Pennsylvania, County Marriages, 1885 - 1950," index and images, FamilySearch, Cataldo Giannoiri and Lina Amica, 1913.

[4] "Italy, Caltanissetta, San Cataldo, Civil Registration (Tribunale), 1866-1910." Images.FamilySearch. Entry for Cataldo Giannone, born 26 Oct 1886. Citing Nati (1881 – 1890); digital folder – image 1797 of 3,142 images; Record number 666.

[5] List or Manifest of United States Citizens arriving in New York from Palermo, Italy; 24 January 1910 on the San Giorgio. List number 12, line number 14, for Cataldo Giannone; the record confirming his county of origin, and destination in the United States, accessed in "New York Passenger Lists;" online at Ancestry.com, November 2012.

[6] Pennsylvania Death Index for 1906-1962, Death Index record for Cataldo Giannone, Year: 1919. Record Number 99249. File Name C – D.pdf, page 191 of 291.

[7] Certificate of Death for Cataldo Giannone, Commonwealth of Pennsylvania, Department of Health, File Number 7039678.

[8] Michele never Americanized his name to Michael. Therefore, all references to him retain the Italian spelling.

[9] "Italy, Caltanissetta, Serradifalco, Civil Registration (Tribunale), 1866-1910." Images.FamilySearch. Entry for Michele Aquilina, born 19 March 1888. Citing Nati (1879 – 1898); digital folder – image 1,340 of 3,025 images; Record number 101.

[10] "Italy, Caltanissetta, Serradifalco, Civil Registration (Tribunale), 1866-1910." Images.FamilySearch. Entry for Michele Aquilina and Catalda Geraci, married 8 June 1907. Citing Matrimoni (1887 – 1910); digital folder – image 857 of 1,037 images; Record number 38.

[11] "Italy, Caltanissetta, Serradifalco, Civil Registration (Tribunale), 1866-1910." Images.FamilySearch. Entry for Catalda Geraci, born 12 March 1890. Citing Nati (1879 – 1898); digital folder – image 1,650 of 3,025 images; Record number 118.

[12] List or Manifest of Alien Passengers for the United States arriving in Philadelphia, Pennsylvania from Palermo, Italy; 20 August 1913, on the America. List number 51, line number 1, for Michele Aquilina; the record confirming his Italian origin, last residence in Serradifalco, accessed in "Philadelphia Passenger Lists;" online at Ancestry.com, November 2012.

[13] "Pennsylvania, County Marriages, 1885 - 1950," index and images, FamilySearch. Michele Aquilina and Calogera Giannone, 1923.

[14] "Pennsylvania, County Marriages, 1885-1950," index and images, FamilySearch (https://familysearch.org/pal:/MM9.1.1/KHF5-BJL : accessed 04 Mar 2013), Michele Aquilina and Calogero Geannone, 1923.

[15] List or Manifest of United States Citizens arriving in New York from Palermo, Italy; 9 May 1924 on the Giuseppe Verdi. List number 103, page 19, line number 23 – 25, for Calogero Aquilina, Angelina Aquilina, and Marianna Aquilina; the record confirming their county of origin, and destination in the United States, accessed in "New York Passenger Lists;" online at Ancestry.com, November 2012.

[16] Pennsylvania Department of Health; Online Death Indices; 1906 – 1962, Death Index record for Michele Aquilina, Year: 1940. File Number 6469. File A – B.pdf, page 13 of 273.

[17] From author's interview with Lucille Leonardi Maziarz, May, 2012.

[18] Author's visit to Denison Cemetery in Swoyersville, Pennsylvania. While at the cemetery, I took a photo of Anna Prizzi's marker. The date of death was 15 August 1985.

[19] "Italy, Caltanissetta, San Cataldo, Civil Registration (Tribunale), 1866-1910." Images.FamilySearch. https://familysearch.org : accessed 2013. Entry for Angelo Occhipenti, born 15 March 1898. Citing Nati (1881 – 1890); digital folder – image 2,292 of 3,111 images; Record number 267.

[20] List or Manifest of United States Citizens arriving in New York from Palermo, Italy; 1 June 1903 on the Bolivia. List number 11, line number 26 – 30, Image 9 of 172, for Francesa Napolitano, Maria Occhipenti, Rosa Occhipenti, Antonio Occhipenti, and Angelo Occhipenti; the record confirming their county of origin, and destination in the United States, accessed in "New York Passenger Lists;" online at Ancestry.com, November 2012.

[21] List or Manifest of United States Citizens arriving in New York from Palermo, Italy; 21 June 1909 on the Tomaso Di Savoia. List number 30, line number 19 – 22, Image 436 of 451, for Lucia Ormando, Anthony Prizzi, Anna Prizzi, and Ross Prizzi; the record confirming their county of origin, and destination in the United States, accessed in "New York Passenger Lists;" online at Ancestry.com, November 2012.

[22] "Pennsylvania, County Marriages, 1885-1950," index and images, FamilySearch (https://familysearch.org/pal:/MM9.1.1/KHFF-96Q : accessed 04 Mar 2013), Angelo Oschipinti and Anna Prizzi, 1919.

[23] Records of the Department of Mines and Mineral Industries; Registers Of Mine Accidents For The Anthracite Districts, 1899-1972. {series #45.14}; Pennsylvania State Archives,

Bureau of Archives and History, Pennsylvania Historical and Museum Commission; File name – Surnames Beginning with "O"; http://www.phmc.state.pa.us/bah/dam/rg/di/r45_MineAccidentRegisters/OsAnthracite19 33_1972.pdf; Accessed 3 March 2013.

[24] William C. Kashatus, "White Haven Center brings decades of experience;" *Citizen's Voice,* 13 June 2010.

[25] "Pennsylvania, County Marriages, 1885 - 1950," index and images, FamilySearch, Stephen L Bellanca and Nellie Defrancesco, 1946.

[26] "Bellanca Doing Well," *The Sunday Independent* (Wilkes-Barre, PA), October 18, 1953, sec. D, 18.

[27] "Asks Support for Heart Fund," *The Sunday Independent* (Wilkes-Barre, PA), February 22, 1953, sec. D, 9.

[28] "Auto Kills Woman near Harding Home," *The Times Leader*, April 24, 1958, sec A, 16.

[29] Ancestry.com, Social Security Death Index; Number: 207-01-2121; Issue State: Pennsylvania; Issue Date: Before 1951.

[30] List or Manifest of United States Citizens arriving in New York from Palermo, Italy; 21 June 1909 on the Tomaso Di Savoia. List number 30, line number 19 – 22, Image 436 of 431, for Lucia Ormando, Anthony Prizzi, Anna Prizzi and Ross Prizzi; the record confirming their county of origin, and destination in the United States, accessed in "New York Passenger Lists;" online at Ancestry.com, November 2012.

[31] Pennsylvania County Marriages, 1885 - 1950, "Pennsylvania, County Marriages, 1885 - 1950," index and images, FamilySearch (https://familysearch.org/pal:/MM9.1.1/VF7Z-TGP : accessed 12 Sep 2012), Ross B. Prizzi and Elizabeth A. Biscontine, 1934.

[32] In 1970 the Scranton Philharmonic and Wilkes-Barre Philharmonic joined to form the Northeastern Pennsylvania Philharmonic.

[33] Social Security Death Index; Decedent's Name – Ross Prizzi; Number: 207-01-7178; Issue State: Pennsylvania; *Ancestry.com*. http://www.ancestry.com; accessed Oct 2012.

[34] Obituary for Ross Prizzi; *Times Leader*; Wilke-Barre;16 May 1996; Genealogybank.com; http://www.genealogybank.com (accessed June 2012).

[35] Obituary and Death Notice for Elizabeth Prizzi; Times Leader, Wilkes-Barre; 2 August 1996; Genealogybank.com; http://www.genealogybank.com (accessed June 2012)..

[36] U.S., Department of Veterans Affairs BIRLS Death File, 1850-2010; Record for Tony Amico; Born 3 January 1911; Died 24 January 1982; Enlisted 31 August 1942; Enlisted 27 October 1950; Discharged 22 Oct 1953; Ancestry.com (http://www.ancestry.com); accessed October 2012.

[37] Bud Hughey, "Tony and 'The Great One'…A Story of Pals," The Geneva Times, 8 January 1962, sec. A, 5.

[38] The episode "Brother Ralph" was originally broadcast on 26 November 1955 on CBS.

[39] Ibid.

[40] Social Security Death Index; Decedent's Name – Tony Amico; Number: 158-12-8298; Issue State: New Jersey; *Ancestry.com*. http://www.ancestry.com; accessed Oct 2012.

[41] "Italy, Caltanissetta, San Cataldo, Civil Registration (Tribunale), 1866-1910." Images.FamilySearch. Entry for Concetto Agati, born 11 June 1888. Citing Nati (1881 – 1890); digital folder – image 2,357 of 3,142 images; Record number 371.

[42] List or Manifest of United States Citizens arriving in New York from Palermo, Italy; 24 March 1907 on the Sofia Hohenberg. List number 29, Line number 28, Image 30 of 237, for Concetto Agati; the record confirming his country of origin, and destination in

the United States, accessed in "New York Passenger Lists;" online at Ancestry.com, November 2012.

[43] List or Manifest of United States Citizens arriving in New York from Palermo, Italy; 26 June 1921 on the Duca D Aosta. Line number 12, Image 325 of 406, for Carmelo Agati; the record confirming his country of origin, and destination in the United States, accessed in "New York Passenger Lists;" online at Ancestry.com, November 2012.

[44] "Pennsylvania, County Marriages, 1885 - 1950," index and images, FamilySearch (https://familysearch.org/pal:/MM9.1.1/KHFN-G3Q : accessed 10 Sep 2012), Concetto Agati and Maria Ormando, 1910

[45] "Italy, Caltanissetta, Caltanissetta, Civil Registration (Tribunale), 1866-1910." Images.FamilySearch. Entry for Maria Ormando, born 8 June 1895. Citing Nati (1881 – 1890); digital folder – image 1,476 of 3,111 images; Record number 399.

[46] Pennsylvania Death Index for 1906-1962, Death Index record for Antonino Agati, Page 1541 for the year 1914, Record Number 27388. File Name A – B.pdf, page 12 of 305.

[47] "Italian Club Charter Granted by Court"; Wilkes-Barre Times Leader; Wilkes-Barre; 29 July 1915; Page 15.

[48] List or Manifest of United States Citizens arriving in New York from Palermo, Italy; 14 April 1922, on the Providence. List number 4, Page number 4, line number 3, for Concetto Agati; the record confirming his U.S. citizenship, and residence in the United States, accessed in "New York Passenger Lists;" online at Ancestry.com, November 2012.

[49] Thomas Hunt and Michael A. Tona, *"Men of Montedoro." Informer - History of American Crime and Law Enforcement, no. 3*, Connecticut, 2012, page 18

[50] Ibid, page 18

[51] Pennsylvania Death Index for 1906-1962, Death Index record for Frank Agati, http://www.health.state.pa.us/indices, Record Number 21360. File A – B.pdf, page 12 of 320.

[52] "District Organizer Slain in Cappellini's Office," *Wilkes-Barre Record*, Wilkes-Barre; 23 February 1928

[53] "Band, 121 Automobiles in Agaty Funeral Cortege," *Wilkes-Barre Record,* Wilkes-Barre; 24 February 1928.

[54] "Guilty of Manslaughter;" *Kingston Daily Freeman*; Kingston, New York; 14 April 1928; page 7.

[55] "Deaths"; Wilkes-Barre Times Leader; (Wilkes-Barre, PA); 7 February 1913; Page 10.

[56] Pennsylvania Department of Health; Online Death Indices; 1906 – 1962, Death Index record for Mary Maloney, Year: 1919. File Number 8015. File Name: D-19 M-N-O.pdf. Page 22 of 354.

[57] 1920 U.S. Federal Census, Pittston City, Luzerne, Pennsylvania, ED 159, Sheet 17B, Dwelling 281, Family 310, Patrick Maloney household, digital image, Ancestry.com. http://www.ancestry.com; accessed November 2012..

[58] "Pennsylvania, County Marriages, 1885-1950," index and images, FamilySearch (https://familysearch.org/pal:/MM9.1.1/KHFW-CY5 : accessed 04 Mar 2013), William Maloney and Mary E De Lorenzo, 1939.

[59] National Institutes of Health, "Glomerulonephritis, 2011," under "Medline Plus," http://www.nlm.nih.gov/medlineplus/ency/article/000484.htm (accessed 13 April 2013).

[60] Ibid.

[61] Pennsylvania Historical and Museum Commission; Harrisburg, Pennsylvania; Pennsylvania Veterans Burial Cards, 1929-1990; Archive Collection Number: Series 3; Folder Number: 787; *Ancestry.com*. http://www.ancestry.com; accessed Oct 2012.

[62] "Pennsylvania, County Marriages, 1885-1950," index and images, FamilySearch (https://familysearch.org/pal:/MM9.1.1/KHF8-5Y3 : accessed 04 Mar 2013), William A Maloney and Rose Mary DiLorenzo, 1946.

[63] Pennsylvania Death Index for 1906-1962, Death Index record for Angelo DiLorenzo, http://www.health.state.pa.us/indices, Record Number 99249. File C – D.pdf, page 215 of 258.

[64] U.S., Department of Veterans Affairs BIRLS Death File, 1850-2010. Ancestry.com, Death Record for Catal Ormando; *Ancestry.com*. http://www.ancestry.com; accessed Oct 2012.

[65] Social Security Death Index; Number – 192-24-4493; Issue State: Pennsylvania; Decedent's Name – Rose Ormando; Ancestry.com (http://www.ancestry.com); accessed Oct 2012.

[66] "Pennsylvania, County Marriages, 1885-1950," index and images, FamilySearch (https://familysearch.org/pal:/MM9.1.1/KHFS-7VS : accessed 04 Mar 2013), Catal Ormando and Rose M Keating, 1934.

[67] 1940 U.S. Federal Census, Wilkes-Barre, Luzerne, Pennsylvania, ED 290, Sheet 63A, Visited Number 306, Peter Carroll household, digital image, Ancestry.com. http://www.ancestry.com; accessed November 2012.

[68] "Pennsylvania, County Marriages, 1885-1950," index and images, FamilySearch (https://familysearch.org/pal:/MM9.1.1/KHFZ-YTH : accessed 04 Mar 2013), Catal James Ormando and Anna Kerchanin, 1945.

[69] "Last Week," *Sunday Independent*, 31 March 1946, Wilkes-Barre, Pennsylvania, sec. C-10.

[70] "Pennsylvania, County Marriages, 1885-1950," index and images, FamilySearch (https://familysearch.org/pal:/MM9.1.1/KHF6-W7H : accessed 04 Mar 2013), Catal James Ormando and Anna Kerchanin, 1947.

[71] U.S., Department of Veterans Affairs BIRLS Death File, 1850-2010; Decedent's Name: Catal Ormando; *Ancestry.com*. http://www.ancestry.com; accessed Oct 2012.

[72] Obituary and Death Notice for Anna Ormando; Times Leader, Wilkes-Barre; 3 May 2001.

[73] "Maziarz Sure to Give Democrats Real Service," *Sunday Independent*, Wilkes-Barre, 6 August 1950.

[74] Lucille was still a minority owner in the ZOM Construction Company in 2013, some 49 years later.

Chapter 8 - Remains

[75] Marble, Page 89.

[76] My cousins, siblings, and I used to play in that very backyard in the 1960s and 1970s.

Chapter 9 - Epilogue

[77] The other was Lucy Agati (1913 – 1995). Although Grace DiLorenzo also never married, she was only 22 when she died.

Made in the USA
Lexington, KY
09 July 2013